A BEDSIDE BOOK OF
ENGLISH SAINTS AFTER 1066

Other Bedside Books

★

A BEDSIDE BOOK OF
ENGLISH SAINTS
AFTER 1066

BY

ALOYSIUS ROCHE

LONDON
BURNS OATES & WASHBOURNE
1948

NIHIL OBSTAT: GEORGIVS CAN. SMITH, S.T.D., PH.D.
CENSOR DEPVTATVS

IMPRIMATVR: E. MORROGH BERNARD
VICARIVS GENERALIS

WESTMONASTERII: DIE XXVIII IVNII MCMXLVII

PRINTED IN GREAT BRITAIN AT THE UNIVERSITY PRESS, ABERDEEN
FOR BURNS OATES AND WASHBOURNE LTD.
28 ASHLEY PLACE
LONDON, S.W.I

First published 1948

CONTENTS

DECLARATION

In conformity with the decree of Pope Urban VIII, dated March 17, 1625, we declare that if in the course of this work we should give the name of Saint to those not officially recognized as such, and if we make mention of such facts and revelations as might bear the character of the miraculous or prophetic, we do not in any way presume to take upon ourselves to express, on either persons or facts, a judgement which is reserved to the Church, nor in any way whatsoever to forecast decisions which belong to her alone.

PENUMBRA

THIS second *Bedside Book of English Saints* attempts to complete what the first began, so that the two volumes together may provide a sort of bird's-eye view of the national sanctity, in so far as that sanctity has been more or less formally acclaimed by the Catholic Church. The Martyrs—that is to say, those men and women who suffered for the old faith in the Reformation period—have been brought into the picture, because they could not well be left out. But, since these are in a class by themselves, and one demanding a treatment outside the scope of a sketch of this kind, they have been dealt with rather summarily.

In the main, our present investigation covers a period of about four hundred years, and is restricted to thirty or forty individuals. Obviously, therefore, we must make the most of those we have, even to the extent of padding them out somewhat with contemporary history. This can be done without over-laboured ingenuity, because all without exception were spectators of great events. As for those amongst them who were public characters or men of affairs, they bring their padding along with them. If their *Lives* read like State Papers, this is explained by the fact that, in those days, Spiritual and Temporal were closely knit, the one serving and, on occasions, attempting to encroach upon the other. English churchmen have an exceptionally fine record as civil servants. With few exceptions, they conducted the business of the nation without detriment to their ecclesiastical dignity or decency, while several of them reached a high degree of sanctity in spite of the fact that they were the keepers at once of the King's Conscience and of the Great Seal.

And we must take them as we find them, if we are to interest ourselves in them at all. When Diderot, the French philosopher, was presented with a portrait of his father in which the painter had represented the worthy cutler of Langres in his best coat and wig,

I

the son declared : " This is my Sunday father : I want my every-day father." Regrettably enough, in the chronicles and bio-graphies, some of these saints seem to be wearing their best clothes all the time, and all their days look like Sundays. The persons are apt to be swallowed up by the personages. After 1066 we get saints and great saints, but for the most part they seem different from their predecessors. The difference is like that between the *Magnificat* and the *Te Deum*. Each is a great hymn of praise and thanksgiving, and each is in a class by itself. The *Te Deum* is a thing of grandeur, but the *Magnificat* excels for sweetness and simplicity as, of course, is to be expected considering whose were the lips that pronounced it for the first time. The Norman Conquest stripped the English of some of their more homely attributes ; while, at the same time, the conquerors adorned the kingdom with men eminent in Church and State. Hence, although there is a fundamental continuity about the sanctity, the more intimate elements are inclined to recede in favour of the formal and the official.

At either end of the survey, and serving as landmarks, we have St. Wulstan, Bishop of Winchester, and John de Tweng, Prior of Bridlington in Yorkshire. The latter, who renounced an academic career at Oxford in order to become a Canon Regular and a con-templative, died in 1379 and, with him, this realm ceased to make good until the cause of the aforesaid Martyrs was taken in hand in recent times.

Landmarks indeed !

Wulstan lived long enough to see the old Anglo-Saxon order in process of liquidation ; John of Bridlington lived long enough to see the social and religious structure of his country threatened by disruptive forces of various kinds. The bishop was born in 1006, a year terrible for England, when Sweyn of Denmark carried fire and sword over the greater part of the country, being bought-off for the time being by a contribution of £30,000 in gold The prior was a contemporary of William Langland, whose hero, Piers Plowman, had a vision of Christ, our Saviour, walking through

English fields dressed as a common labourer; and he died on the very eve of the social insurrection associated with the names of Jack Straw, John Ball and Wat Tyler which marked the decline and fall of feudalism.

Within the picturesque horizon stretching between these two lie the Middle Ages proper, that is to say, the Middle Ages full-blooded and matured. And since each period of time has its own special character, we must expect these saints to be what they were, one hundred per cent. medievalists. It was within the framework of medieval conceptions of life, of politics, of society and of religion that their sanctification was worked out. For better and for worse, for richer and for poorer, their milieu affected their outlook, mentality and actions. We find ourselves here in the midst of anathemas, suspensions and interdicts. We find folk being excommunicated right and left; and surviving it too. The Middle Ages had these things somewhat on the brain; at any rate, so it must seem to those who have ceased to take religious questions very seriously.

"Even the best poetry, when it is at all personal, needs the penumbra of its own time, place and circumstances to make it full and whole." It sounds reasonable enough. And may we not make the same claim for personal holiness? Our goodness is a reflexion of God's and, therefore, a divine revelation. But the light of this revelation is differently reflected in the prism of each age, and assumes a form determined by the age. Hence we must be prepared to find these saints circumscribed and influenced, not only by their own temperament, but by the temperament of the times in which they lived.

Undoubtedly, the five centuries that intervene between the Conquest and the accession of Queen Elizabeth are some folk's pet aversion. But a pet aversion is bound to make us unfair in our estimation of periods and persons. We judge even the living on insufficient evidence as a rule, since some vital clue to their make-up is hidden from us. Still, just as we may, suddenly—all in a flash so to say—acquire an insight into the true character of those with whom we imagine ourselves to be well acquainted, so it is sometimes granted to our glance to reach beyond the superficial ugliness of an age to its real core. This is a saving grace, and like other graces ought not to be resisted. And, surely, at the core of medieval life lay the memory of Redemption, of the debt contracted by the human race on Mount Calvary. This memory mingled with everything and was to be found in all institutions, in all monuments and, at certain moments, in all hearts.

Not only are we under the influence of a reaction against the medieval environment—and in many ways quite justifiably so—but we are apt to interpret everything in it in terms of everything in our own, to thrust upon it our particular ways of thinking. And thus, we may forget that what we call the dream of the Holy Roman Empire was one that haunted the medieval mind just as, at the moment, some minds among us are haunted by the dream of a World Federation. And dream or no dream, the importance of the Holy Roman Empire in history is enormous. Into it all the life of the ancient world was gathered ; out of it all the life of the modern world arose.

Always when human society reaches any decisive stage of development, those at the top naturally apply their minds to the vital matter of securing for it some sort of stability and permanence. It was so in the Greece of Plato's time, when that great man envisaged his Republic as a kind of celestial state realized here upon earth. The Middle Ages had a similar vision. They were inspired by the idea of a Theocracy as the one practical solvent of all political and social problems. This it is that explains much in the behaviour of the Church which, to us, appears so high-handed and even harsh. But we must measure her responsibility not merely by what she did, but also by what she was working for and was up against.

If, therefore, the medieval Church appears to be somewhat callous in sacrificing the individual to the species, after the fashion of nature, it may well be that this becomes necessary at certain stages ; when anarchy threatens the whole, the parts must submit to restraint and restriction. Had it not been for a rigid discipline and authority, the Christian religion, in that turbulent period, might have become the mere plaything of contemporary social and political upheavals. Then, more than ever, was it imperative that, in the one place where men and women were united in striving after a moral ideal, they should be habituated to rule and law. Nor must it be overlooked that, in the view of the Catholic Church, Christianity is not only a doctrine and a life, but also a society, complete with its own juridical and institutional organization. Hence those attributes and appendages so repugnant to the naïve and bucolic type of religionist—pomp, power and prestige; hence the officiousness and seeming arrogance of saints like Thomas Becket and Edmund Rich.

Then, again, if these saints seem to be for ever quarrelling, we may charitably believe that this was their trial as it was their providential lot. St. Francis of Assisi had no quarrels to speak of, except with the Wolf of Gubbio. But, then, his vocation did not lie in that direction. "God has summoned me to the conflict," Gregory the Great said when he was elected Pope. And God does summon some people to these conflicts. His own divine Son was a sign of contradiction. These contentions may exhibit the participants in rather an unattractive light, but it is extremely doubtful if mere placid amiability will get any of us canonized.

There is this much to be said for these quarrels and these quarrelsome people; to them we owe many of our cherished liberties. There seems to be no doubt that the Anglo-Norman rulers were far more tyrannical than their Anglo-Saxon predecessors; if some of them had had their way, the people would have been devoured like so much bread. And there is no doubt at all that, in the conflicts carried on between Church and State, the people sided in the main with the ecclesiastics. We see this even in the case of a measure so extreme as the Interdict. This was Pope Innocent's masterstroke directed against the iniquities of King John who, when it was threatened, swore by God's teeth —his favourite oath—that, as a reprisal, he would amputate the ears and nose of every single Italian resident within the nation. But the blow fell for all that; and for some years the bells were silent, the altars stripped, the images covered up, the laity excluded from each and every church service. All religious rites were refused except baptism to new-born infants and viaticum to the dying. Marriages were celebrated in the church yards. Some of the clergy wavered and gave in, but these few were looked upon by the people as traitors who had sacrificed their conscience to their temporal interests. It was, in fact, a popular interdict; and it succeeded, as much as anything, in convincing the king that his behaviour was an object of universal hatred.

At the same time, let it not be too easily assumed that this epoch was the Golden Age of ecclesiastical domination. It is doubtful if the Catholic Church has ever seen her authority more contested in practice, even by those who recognised it in theory. As we shall see, where that authority was thought to be abusive, it was contested very hotly indeed by some of our saints, for example, in the matters of papal taxation and of Italian encroachment upon our benefices and emoluments. Church officials certainly multiplied in this country as elsewhere, but is there any evidence to show that these stood apart from the nation in the guise of an exclusive and tyrannical caste? Of Chaucer's company who travelled to Canterbury, no less than seven belonged to the ecclesiastical establishment—the Prioress, the Monk, the Friar, the Clerk, the Parson, the Summoner and the Pardoner. But they are on easy terms with the others, and take their turn in telling a story. It is the host of the Tabard Inn who is the director or president. Good companions all—that is what they are, bound together by a fellowship in which there is neither arrogance nor servility, no haughtiness and no reserve.

A strictly impartial view of this period is probably beyond the power of most of us. However anxious we may be to get at the bare facts of ancient history, we can only understand them by bringing them into relation with our own mind. But this mind is not an empty mind; it is one furnished with personal categories and prejudices, and therefore disposed to look at things in a particular way. To be entirely just in our judgement of the past is, then, not difficult, but impossible ; but we can at least make the attempt.

In the case of an age so remote from ours in almost every way, the effort involved may be prodigious. To reproduce the atmosphere of a given time and place so vividly that it can be breathed in at a breath is an artistic achievement of no mean order, the achievement of painters and writers of genius. Emily Brontë, to give one instance, not only felt the essential soul of the Yorkshire moor, but she was able to convey the sense of it in phrase after phrase. For this is she deservedly praised, although she had the advantage of being actually steeped in the thing whose realization she was passing on to us. But, even with all the good will in the world, how can we be expected to feel the pulse of the twelfth and thirteenth centuries ? Between us and them there lies a gulf of separation and of difference which the prose of the most conscientious historian can hardly bridge over. The floor of heaven, to them so near, has since receded to an immeasurable distance ; the very earth, which they pictured as huge and preponderating, we conceive of as a mere speck in the awful vastness of the spheres. And these transformations are symbolic of others more intimate and more profound. The whole fabric of custom and habit which they so laboriously built for themselves has crumbled long since. They cannot come to us ; our imagination and sympathy can but feebly penetrate to them. Such hints and tokens as we have are but faint echoes out of a vanished world.

If we are to approach to impartiality we must endeavour to be complete. It is not impartiality to shut one eye, no matter how keen and penetrating may be the glance of the eye that is kept open. To portray only the vices or the virtues of a human being is not biography ; and to exhibit only the bad or the good of a given period is not history. The type of Catholic who idealizes everything in these times, and the type of anti-Catholic who anathematizes everything in them are equally astray, although in different directions. A landscape of sheer beauty, sunlit and resplendent, with women here and there splendidly dressed and all very good-looking; then, in the midst of all, the fair form of the Church rising up and expanding like a summer pageant from north to south—majestic, solemn, bright, soothing to the griefs and indulgent to the hopes of the population. A brotherhood of holy pastors with mitre and crozier and uplifted hand, walks forth to bless and rule a joyful people. The crucifix heads the procession of simple unworldly monks, their hearts in prayer, and of choir-boys with faces like cherubs—high festival and plaintive dirge and passing bell and the twilight call to vespers. In short, heaven let down upon the earth and that earth no other than the countryside that Chaucer knew and William Langland. This is one picture.

The other is that of an empty, ugly chasm lying between two very fine periods of civilization, in which European man lies gagged and bound and given over to rank ignorance and superstition, a noxious miasma blown away at last by the virginal breath of Good Queen Elizabeth.

Neither picture is a portrait. At that date, the nations of our continent were not indeed in their infancy, for they were surrounded and influenced by ancient institutions. But neither were they adults, for that title cannot be applied either to individuals or to societies until they attain a definite development. What we find amongst them is neither the height of civilization nor the depth of barbarism, but a mixture of the two.

Contradictions entered into everything, even into the sacred precincts of religious practice. Wrong-doers never fancied that God could be discounted, but they rather toyed with the notion that He might be adroitly side-tracked or even hoodwinked. It is said that Richard the First stayed away from Confession for seven years in order to avoid the painful necessity of having to forgive Philip of France. Again, during the Becket dispute, Henry found himself under the same roof as his opponent, and with no option but to assist at the Mass to be celebrated the following morning. Piety required that, during the celebration, the king should, as usual, receive the kiss of peace from the archbishop, a gesture which would not have suited his mood or policy at all. Casuistry came to the rescue. It was arranged that the Mass should be one for the dead in which the kiss of peace is always omitted. Later on, the primate's assassins, one of whom it is alleged had received the Sacrament of Holy Order, and all of whom were certainly baptized Catholics, tried to drag him from the church, in order, presumably, to avoid committing two sins of sacrilege instead of one.

And with regard even to the saints now under review—and indeed to saints generally—we are reminded by one of the Fathers of the church that not all their actions are equally holy. The Stoics of old desiderated in their pattern men a total absence of passions and of weaknesses ; but the saints, thank God, are not fashioned in so leaden a mould. There is this consideration besides ; no matter how disedifying may be the outward history of God's Kingdom on earth, in this or that age, there is ever an inward or spiritual history which acts, in some measure, as a corrective and compensation. Bearing in mind that it is not always easy for us to justify the ways of God to men, we shall not take it amiss if, sometimes, we find it difficult to justify the ways of certain men to God.

It is just as well, too, to make a clean breast of it and record here that the whole procession marches to the tune of innumerable prodigies, although space forbids anything like their detailed enumeration. In that far off time, the devil was a formidable reality. " Your adversary goeth about as a roaring lion "—they had excellent authority for believing that ; and they did believe it. They rang their church bells to avert lightning and tempest, blight and famine ; for they persuaded themselves that these were due to diabolical agency. Satan was " the prince of the powers of the air " and so the air was set vibrating in order to shake him out of his kingdom. Recruiting for the Crusades went ahead to the accompaniment of heavenly manifestations. A comet appeared of great brilliancy and shaped like a sword; some working in the fields reported that they had seen the image of a great city suspended in the sky; a priest of honourable reputation beheld two spectral knights who met one another in the air and fought, until the one who carried a cross struck the other and grounded him for good and all. As for miracles, no fewer than four hundred and twenty-nine were put forward in support of Thomas of Hereford's cause, while those collected on behalf of Henry the Sixth's canonization filled a goodly volume—*The Book of the King's Miracles*. The invisible world constituted the basis or background of the bulk of the literature and art of the Middle Ages.

Very predisposed indeed were those people to believe in the supernatural. But, let it be whispered low, the average Catholic (the writer included) is still inclined that way, at any rate to the extent that he or she would rather believe than not believe. The medievalists, however, were ready to stake their faith on a hundred to one chance. They armed themselves with credulity as with a weapon and, by its means, chased the Evil One down the vista of their own damnable doubts.

THE TRANSITION

Sixty years after Hastings, William the monk of Malmesbury describes the battle as " a fatal day " for England. " Melancholy havoc," he goes on, " was wrought in our dear country during the changes of its lords. Long before, it had adopted the manners of the Angles, who at first were barbarians, warlike in their usages, heathen in their rites. But, after embracing the faith of Christ, by degrees they relegated arms to a second place and gave their whole attention to religion. What shall I say of the multitude of their bishops, hermits and abbots ? Does not the whole island blaze with such numerous relics that you can scarcely pass a village but you hear the name of some new saint ? And of how many more has all remembrance perished through the want of records ? Nevertheless, religious fervour had decreased for several years before the arrival of the Normans. The clergy were illiterate, the monks worldly and gluttonous, the nobility luxurious and wanton. However, this was by no means true of the English generally. Many of the clergy at that day trod the path of sanctity ; and divers laity, of all ranks and conditions, were well pleasing to God, so that my accusation does not involve the whole indiscriminately."

So much for the conquered. As to the conquerors, saints there may have been in William's *entourage*, but only one of them has been canonized, Osmund, Bishop of Old Sarum, now Salisbury. The administrative body which he set up in his own cathedral became a pattern for the whole country, and was destined to survive into modern times. He it was who put together the Sarum Use or Order of church services, and this came to be adopted not only in England, but in Wales, Ireland and Scotland. We are told that he was free from ambition, neither wasting his own substance nor coveting the wealth of others. We are told again that his virtues were so patent that not even professional slanderers could question them without blushing. Lanfranc has been listed as a saint; but contemporaries were divided as to his title-deeds, and no marks of honour were paid to his memory either at Caen, Bec or Canterbury.

The sanguinary drama of the Conquest was so far from being presented in one act that for a long time invaders and invaded were engaged in constant hostilities. The battle of Hastings really lasted for about seven years. The result of final success was that the greater portion of the lands changed hands; that is to say, as far as ownership was concerned, for, in many cases, the old proprietor became the tenant of the new over-lord. At the end of William's reign, there was not a single English earl, no more than one English bishop and only a few English abbots. What the ordinary people had to endure can be gathered from the extreme instance of the planting of the New Forest, the biggest eviction in our history, when the whole of south-west Hampshire from Salisbury to the sea was depopulated, an area ninety miles in circumference and containing thirty parish churches.

By means of Doomsday Book alone, we can estimate the damage and decay that were the immediate effects of the revolution, an assessment tragically reminiscent of the calamities of our own times. The city of York is set down as containing only 967 homes in a fit state to be inhabited, as against 1607 less than twenty years before. One entire ward of the city is described as having been totally destroyed. Lincoln had lost over two hundred dwellings, Dorchester one hundred, Oxford nearly five hundred, Derby one hundred, Ipswich three hundred and twenty-eight.

Although Holinshed was an Elizabethan writing some five centuries after the event, his account of the harshness of the Conqueror is really a condensation of contemporary chronicles. "He raised great taxes and subsidies through the realm; nor anything regarded the English nobility, so that they who before thought themselves to be made forever by bringing a stranger into the land, did now see themselves trodden under foot, to be despised and mocked on all sides. Many refusing to sustain the intolerable yoke laid upon them, chose rather to quit everything and as outlaws to betake themselves to the woods with their families, meaning thenceforth to live as raiders and highwaymen."

Four saints belong to this turbulent period of transition, to wit Berthold, Stephen Harding, Margaret and Wulstan. All of these were Anglo-Saxons; and all of them were, to some extent, victims of Norman tyranny.

For a considerable period after 1066, the Conqueror's influence was confined to the south of England, so that those amongst the Anglo-Saxon nobility who were disaffected, or suspected of being so, were able to make good their escape from the country without very much difficulty. You had only to make for one of the sea-ports in East Anglia or farther north, and there would be ships and crews in plenty at your disposal.

Many who could afford to do so took advantage of this providential outlet, amongst them the parents of St. Berthold. Arriving safely on the Continent, they traversed Germany and eventually settled down in Parma. St. Berthold was born in that city just about the time when its fine cathedral was completed. In his youth, he entered a monastery, where he died at an early age and where his relics are preserved to this day. Under the circumstances, it was doubtless to be expected that the name and memory of this young monk should be ignored on this side; but he deserves a place in this record, since he has the distinction of being the very first of our countrymen to be canonized in post-Conquest times. He might well be invoked as the patron of displaced persons of whom there are so many at this moment of writing.

Another political exile is St. Stephen Harding, part founder of the Cistercian Order. At the time of the Conquest he was still in his teens; and, we are told, that desiring to try the monastic life, he travelled from Dorset to Scotland, at that time the rallying-point of the Saxon race from the power of the Conqueror. From Scotland, he passed over to the Continent and eventually settled down in France.

St. Margaret was related to Edward the Confessor, to Ethelred the Unready, and to Edmund Ironside, the king renowned for his prodigious bodily strength. She was English enough, therefore, although her country disowned her, in a way, twice over. The tradition is that her father, Edward the Exile, had to flee for safety to Hungary where she may have been born, although the date of her birth is not known for certain. On the accession of the Confessor, she was invited back and arrived safely in London with her father and brother. After the battle of Hastings, many would have liked to have raised this brother to the throne, but failing to sustain his claim by arms he submitted to the Normans. However, knowing well the kind of people he was dealing with, Edgar, the Aethling or Prince, took sail and made good his escape. The ship being driven by a storm upon the coast of Scotland, the King of that country, Malcolm by name and the son of Duncan, welcomed the exiles to his court. In the year 1070, when she was about twenty-four, Margaret and Malcolm were married.

Wulstan's, or Wolstan's, case is by contrast quite a pleasant one. He was a native of Warwickshire, and both his parents entered the cloister in late life. Beginning as a monk at Worcester, where he was expert in teaching children, he was made bishop of that place and became equally expert in suppressing the slave-trade, particularly at Bristol. He had his own opinion about the Conquest for, when folk complained of the oppression of the Normans, he told them that they were the scourges or vermin sent by God for their trial and purification. This Benedictine was the last English bishop appointed under a Saxon ruler, the last representative of the traditions of Bede and Cuthbert—a sort of link connecting the old with the new.

His deposition was demanded on the score, it was said, that he was ignorant, which probably meant not much more than that he was unacquainted with the French tongue and manners. It was, of course, William's policy to weed out all bishops and abbots suspected of being unfavourable to himself. Indeed, it is asserted hat in this he was backed up by Lanfranc, although Lanfranc's chief concern seems to have been to have capable men at the head of ecclesiastical affairs. It is asserted again that the newcomers took steps to drive the Anglo-Saxon saints out of favour. At any rate, there was a good deal of this weeding out.

But Wulstan was not to be got rid of so easily, or got rid of at all. His surely was a case of the meek possessing the earth. It is Aelred of Rievaulx who tells the story. When the good bishop was summoned to Westminster, examined, and called upon by Lanfranc to resign, he stood up and spoke as follows:

" I am aware, my Lord Archbishop, that I am neither worthy of this dignity, nor equal to its duties: this I knew when the clergy elected me, when the prelates compelled me to accept the dignity, when my master Edward the Confessor called me to fill it. By the authority of the Holy See, he laid this burden upon me and with this staff he commanded me to receive the rank of a bishop. But you now demand of me the pastoral staff which you did not present, and the office which you did not bestow. Aware of my insufficiency and obedient to this holy synod, I now resign them—not, however, to you but to him by whose authority I received them."

He then laid his crozier upon the tomb of the Confessor and took his seat among the monks as a simple member of their order. Some say that the crozier remained embedded in the tomb and could not be moved. Others affirm that the synod was ashamed to enforce the resignation after Wulstan's speech. One way or the other, he was not molested.

With all respect to this imposing commission and its findings, Wulstan was a model bishop. Without any great learning, he devoted his long life to the care of his flock, visiting, preaching and confirming without cessation. He rebuilt his cathedral in the simple Saxon style, planted new churches wherever they were needed, and retained to the last the unworldly and ascetic habits he had acquired in his monastery. Prayerful and recollected, the psalms were for ever on his lips, and he recited the divine office aloud with his attendants as he rode up and down his diocese.

There was something of the Pied Piper about him, too, for children left their very food to run after him. He would go fasting from sunrise to sunset in order to bless batch after batch of these little ones who thronged about his horse. He was respected by the highest in the land. King Harold is reported to have travelled as much as thirty miles in order to make his confession to Wulstan. The Conqueror esteemed him; and John, who was perhaps the worst ruler England ever had, was laid to rest by his side. He was nearly ninety when he died, survived both William and Lanfranc, and lived to assist at the consecration of St. Anselm.

As to the charge of illiteracy brought against the native clergy by the usurpers, it may be conceded that the education of many had been sadly neglected. But that this very same charge was valid in the case of some of the Normans themselves can be gathered from the record of a visitation made, later on, by the Archbishop of Rouen. "The same day, we examined Godfrey, a clerk, who had been presented to the church of St. Richard of Herecourt. Taking the passage *Omnia autem aperta et nuda sunt ejus oculis* (All things are open and naked before His eyes), we asked what part of speech *aperta* was; he replied 'a noun.' Asked whether it could be any other part, he replied 'Yes, a participle.' Asked what *pateo* meant, he said 'to open or to suffer.' Asked what part of speech *absque* was, he said it was a conjunction; asked of what kind, he said 'causal'."

There was much more in the same strain, so that Godfrey was plucked.

With regard to the cause of all these troubles, if we are to believe contemporary accounts, the Conqueror was somewhat remorseful when the end came, although his death was singularly peaceful and, in a way, edifying. Having made some tardy restitutions, at sunrise on September 9th, 1087, he was roused from a stupor by the pealing of the bells of Rouen. He inquired what the sound meant and was told that they were ringing the hour of Prime in the church of St. Mary. Thereupon, he lifted his hands to heaven and said: " I recommend my soul to my lady

Mary the holy mother of God." And so he expired. A monkish historian relates the sequel. "Seeing him depart, the wealthiest of his attendants mounted their horses and galloped off to secure their property. But the others laid hands on the plate, robes, linen and furniture, and left the corpse almost naked on the floor. Observe then, I pray you, my readers, how little trust can be placed in human fidelity." How little indeed !

ANOTHER KIND OF FUGITIVE

THE anchorite is literally one who beats a retreat, a proceeding which may or may not be cowardice. There are such things as strategic retreats. And that is just how the word is understood in the Christian vocabulary. *Convolate ad urbes refugii*—fly to the cities of refuge! Thus of old did the monks exhort perspective candidates outside. The hermit flies a little farther, that is all. He or she is one who seeks to overcome flesh and devil by depriving them of their partner the world; weakening the Triple Alliance by a third.

The newly-converted Anglo-Saxons had a great partiality for this manner of living whose attraction many of their most active churchmen were never able to shake off. After the Conquest, solitaries so multiplied that the place-name Armitage was not uncommon. There is still an Armitage near Rugeley in Staffordshire, the word being derived from the old French *hermitage*. They so multiplied, in fact, that eventually proper manuals of instruction were written for their use, one of which—as we shall see—takes its place in our literature as a real classic.

It has been noted how the change-over of 1066 produced a multitude of those whom we, nowadays, are only too familiar with under the name of displaced persons. Of these, some retired into the more inaccessible parts of the kingdom and fought bravely and for long against the encroachments of the invaders. Hereward the Wake, *England's Darling*, was of this number. Others, again, banded themselves together and preyed upon the possessions of their new masters. Robin Hood, if he existed at all, belonged to this class. But there were many whose only desire was to live in such peace as might enable them to say their prayers and prepare for death. Before long, these were to be found in every part of the country. Their religious character secured for them the respect of everybody, the Norman settlers included. There were

Bridge Hermits, Forest Hermits and Fen Hermits. In Derbyshire there were cave dwellers or *spelotai*. Robert of Knaresborough lived this life as late as the thirteenth century. With the dying down of the political turmoil, many emerged from their retreats and took up useful employments. Some acted as caretakers of leper houses, others lived near the great highways which they kept in a state of repair. Others again looked after the tolls as, for instance, in London at Aldgate, Bishopsgate, Cripplegate and Charing Cross. We even hear of them as custodians of our primitive lighthouses; at Tynemouth, Farne Island, Lynn, Skegness, Reculver, St. Alban's Head, Plymouth, Dover and St. Catherine's Down in the Isle of Wight.

Small islands were favoured by quite a number. Windermere, Thorney and Athelney had their *insulani*. St. Henry of Northumberland lived alone on Coquet Island off the coast of that county, having been summoned to do so by a voice from heaven. The date of his death is 1127, and his life was written by the historian Capgrave. St. Elgar was a Devon man who, like St. Patrick, was carried into Ireland. Regaining his freedom, he settled down on the island of Bardsey off the Carnarvon coast. He died about forty years after the Conquest. Another who chose the west country for his hermitage was St. Wulfsi or Wulsi, who was the spiritual adviser of St. Wulstan, Bishop of Worcester.

Of these little is known, but it is otherwise with St. Wulfric or Ulfric. Around his name and memory plenty of legends grew up. His tomb at Haselbury-Plucknett in Somerset and near the border of Dorset was a popular place of pilgrimage. Born near Bristol and trained for the priesthood, his addiction to sport made him a very indifferent pastor. The story goes that his eyes were opened, and opened through the medium of a beggar whom he befriended. "God reward you for your charity!" said the beggar. "Believe me, you will presently quit this fooling and go where you will find rest. And if you persevere, you will join the company of the saints." Soon after, a certain knight offered the stout hunter a cell adjoining the church. In this cell, he did penance to such purpose that he was reduced to skin and bone. Next this skin and bone he wore not a hair shirt but a garment of chain mail. This he was in the habit of trimming with an ordinary pair of scissors as though it had been so much linen. These odds and ends the people carried off and treasured as relics. This trimming was done, it seems, in order to facilitate the practice of making those prostrations which were in vogue at that period. They were of Celtic origin and were practised by St. Thomas Becket and St. Gilbert of Sempringham. In summer and winter alike, Wulfric used to strip to his suit of armour and immerse himself in a bath of cold water. Then he would sing aloud psalms in praise of God. The Cistercians have claimed him as one of their order, but he was unattached.

Most of them were unattached, for that matter. Nowadays such hermits as we have in the Catholic Church belong to one or other of those religious orders which provide for the possibility of their members wanting to lead this kind of life. The Camaldolese, for example, are one such order, and so are the Franciscans ; the inference being that, if the hermit is to be a success, he must first undergo a period of probation in a monastery. But in the Middle Ages there seems to have been no such hard-and-fast procedure. Having made up his mind, the aspirant went through no formality beyond providing himself with a proper garb. Thus, we read that Richard Rolle, the mystic, having resolved to live by himself, straightway took a couple of frocks belonging to his sister and, going into the wood, made himself a suit of hermit's clothes, and from that hour became and was known to be a proper hermit. This same Richard wrote some of his spiritual treatises for the benefit of out-and-out solitaries. St. Simon Stock appears to have been even more forthright, at any rate to the extent of dispensing with the uniform. He received his nickname when he was twelve, at which early age he simply disappeared into the forest lining the bank of the Medway and took to living in the decayed hollow of a great tree. In this eccentricity he persevered for a dozen years, until his solitude was disturbed by the arrival from Palestine of the Carmelite friars, who settled close to his hermitage. Not long after Simon came out of his tree and joined them. The self-same change-over is found also in the life of Robert Flower, the son of a Mayor of York, who began by living in a cavern and finished up as a Trinitarian.

With men up and down the country trying out this experiment, it is not surprising to find the ladies eager to emulate their example. They did so to such purpose that, by the middle of the fourteenth century, quite a considerable number of parish churches had a cell attached harbouring one or other of these anchoresses. Few of their names have survived ; and, although the enterprise had its ups and downs like every enterprise, it appears to have been fairly successful. One thing it did do—and in this one thing it justified itself—it produced a really first-class contemplative. This is Juliana of Norwich, some account of whom will be given in a later chapter. She lived her truly wonderful life in a tiny annexe built into the church of St. Julian in Norwich.

These intrepid women were fortunate, too, in having the support of one of the most attractive personalities of the period. This was he—perhaps Richard Poore, Bishop of Salisbury—who wrote what is by far the most important prose text in early Middle English. It has become customary to refer to this work as the *Ancrene Riwle*, although there is no manuscript authority for this title. But, call it *Riwle* or *Wisse*, it is a directory for female recluses, of which the *Cambridge History of English Literature* says : " Its originality, its personal charm and its sympathy with all that is good in contemporary literature, place it apart as the finest prose work of the time. The writing exhibits astonishing security and ease. This is accomplished, not tentative, prose."

From this masterpiece we gather that there were sometimes three or four of these ladies living under one roof—a high piece of courage at any time. Also that their house usually adjoined the church whose services they could take part in by looking through the open casement. Their *Riwle* is simplicity itself. On rising, they must " visit " the Blessed Sacrament. During the day, they are advised to fall on their knees from time to time and salute the image of our Saviour hanging on His cross. The Office of the Blessed Virgin is recommended, preceded by five Aves and followed by a litany and the Office for the Dead. They must confess their sins to the priest once a week, and receive Holy Communion fifteen times in the year. They must observe the monastic fast from the fourteenth of September until Easter, but during the remainder of the year they may eat twice daily. Their clothing ought to be of coarse texture, but not too coarse, for they are cautioned against wearing hair-cloth or hedgehog skins as undergarments. They may have a maid to wait upon them, go errands and collect whatever alms may be needed for house-keeping. It is evident, however, that for the most part these women belonged to the upper classes and, therefore, lived upon their own patrimony. We gather, besides, that the chief fault found with these recluses was that too many of them failed to restrain their appetite for gossip. The directory quotes the common saying:

> From mill and from market,
> From smithy and from Ancresses' house
> Men bring news.

"Christ knows," comments the Directory, "this is a sorry tale that each ancress should have some old woman or other to feed her ears—a magpie that chatters to her all she hears or sees."

In Lorenzo Lotto's picture of the Annunciation, our Lady's cat is seen scampering to one side with arched back, scared by the sudden entrance of Gabriel, while she kneels by her *prieu-dieu*. It would seem, then, that if secluded and prayerful folk are to have a pet at all, the cat it must be. The dog for the actionist, the cat for the passivist. And this is one big concession which the writer of the *Ancrene Riwle* makes. He authorizes the inmates of the hermitage to keep a cat. If anything will reconcile certain folk to the Middle Ages, surely it is this.

The compiler of the *Ancrene Riwle* is quite candid about the arduous nature of the hermit's calling, even about the difficulty of keeping the " ten old commandments " ; but he remarks that " nothing is ever so hard but that love doth not make it tender and soft and sweet." The most famous solitary of the Anglo-Norman period, St. Godric of Finchale, is an interesting personage in himself, but doubly so as illustrating just this very thing—the opposition, namely, which even the most successful recluse may have to encounter from his or her own restlessness.

This Godric died in 1170, the year of Becket's martyrdom, after having managed to live by himself for very nearly three score years and ten. He comes before us, in the first instance, as a peddler of small wares, pins and ribbons and so forth, which he traded from village to village in an effort to support his needy parents. In due course, like all merchants of that ilk, he improved his stock and began to frequent city markets and fairs. But the hardiest thing of the sort he ever attempted was a voyage to Scotland. He did well, however, and went back again and again. He suffered much from the tongues of the populace, for at that date peddler was another name for rogue. Once it chanced that when he was returning from Scotland, the boat put in at Lindisfarne. Impressed by the look of the island, and by what he heard of the eremitical life led by St. Cuthbert in his last years, he knelt on the spot where that great good man had died and prayed for strength to imitate his example. If anything his petition was too successful, for such strength came to him that he straightway exchanged his merchandise for the staff and cockle-shell of a pilgrim, and made a bee-line for Palestine. Fortunately for him, the Holy Places were at this date in the hands of the Crusaders so that he reached Jerusalem without difficulty.

Our would-be hermit next directed his steps towards Compostella, already famous throughout Christendom as enshrining the tomb and remains of the Apostle St. James the Great. This tradition was already widespread amongst us in the year 700 when our own St. Aldhelm, Bishop of Sherborne, made it the subject of his verse.   But in Godric's time, pilgrims to Compostella had become regular articles of exportation.   Ships were every year fitted out at different ports for their conveyance, while rival tourist agencies canvassed the pious public much as they do now. What is perhaps the earliest extant sea-ballad or chanty deals with this very subject.   It is in a manuscript of the reign of Henry VI, and belongs now to the library of Trinity College, Cambridge.   There are eighteen verses, all flavoured with the popular jargon of seafaring men.   At one time there is a call to the boatswain to " bestow the botte," at another to the steward for a " pot of beere."   During the storm, the passengers have their " bowlys fast theym by."

> Some ladye theyr bookys on theyr kne
> And rad so long they myght nat se.

The pilgrims slept on " saks of strawe " under such close quarters that " a man were as good to be dede, as smell thereof the stynk." The second verse gives us some clue to the points of embarkation.

> For when they have taken the see,
> At Sandwyche or at Wynchylsee,
> At Brystow or where thet hit bee, '
> Theyr herts begyn to fayle.

As for our friend Godric, neither the " saks of strawe " nor the " stynks " could make his " hert begyn to fayle," at least not at this stage.   Returning to his native Norfolk, he did make an attempt to settle down, accepting the post of steward in the family of a rich man.   The attempt was a failure, for almost immediately we find him in France making a pilgrimage to the shrine of one of the chief patron saints of hermits, St. Giles, the same who for years shared a forest life with a hind.   But the intercession of this solitary availed but little, at any rate at the time, for Godric pushed on into Italy until he found himself once again in the Eternal City.   Returning to England, he retired to a desolate place near Carlisle along with a fellow-hermit named Godwin.   However, when this latter died two years later, nothing would do for Godric except to be on the move again. He got as far as Jerusalem but suffered so much, in going and coming, that the *wanderlust* went clean out of his system. Coming home, he tried Whitby first but, finding that seaport too full of painful associations, took up his abode at Finchale or Finkley near Durham. Here, modelling his life on that of Cuthbert and John the Baptist, under whose protection he placed himself, he remained for sixty-three years, the hermit of the running stream, for Finchale is probably " the meadow by the river," this river being the Wear. Once a week, a monk came over from Durham to say Mass and to administer the Sacraments of Penance and the Holy Eucharist. Godric was later confined to his bed ; and the historian, William of Newburgh, who visited him at this time, tells us that though his body appeared to be dead, his tongue never ceased to praise God nor his countenance to retain its dignity and animation. The fame of the miracles he wrought, in life and after death, resounded throughout England.

Meanwhile, we are not to suppose that this sort of life is a thing of the past as far as England is concerned. True, we have no out-and-out anchorites like Henry of Northumberland and Godric of Finchale ; but the inspiration moving people to live like them still subsists, and it is still catered for. There is a Carthusian monastery functioning at this moment near Horsham in Sussex, and the life that goes on inside is essentially eremitical. Each one of these recluses lives in a separate house in which he works and prays and sleeps, all by himself, and which he quits only in order to take part in the common exercises of religion. This Charterhouse has room in its grounds for thirty-six hermits, and is said to be one of the largest in the world.

WHY SO FEW?

THREE dozen swallows are not a great number with which to make a summer. Yet, summer it was in more ways than one. In the Anglo-Saxon period the sun was shining, but there was not much warmth in it; it was the spring-time of our Christian experience. On the other hand, the age of Becket and Edmund Rich and Simon Stock carries a suggestion of ripeness under a blazing sky. There was maturity all round. The general standard of faith and practice was higher. Holiness was more widely diffused. The background was, spiritually, much brighter; and lights have to be very strong if they are to show up against such a background.

Quite a number of illustrious personages there were who conferred great spiritual distinction on this country, and are woven into the very stuff of its medieval history, but they were English saints only in the sense that Disraeli was an English states-man or Goldsmith an English poet. They are the counterparts of the great personages associated with our conversion—Augustine, Paulinus, Mellitus, and so on. It was hard to pass these latter over, hard too to ignore a man like Felix whose episcopal see is now under water. He established many schools, and has had his name coupled with the foundation of Cambridge University. But Felix was a Burgundian, like Hugh of Lincoln in post-Conquest times. It was not easy, either, to cold-shoulder Birinus the first Bishop of Dorchester in the county of Oxford. He is the only saint in these parts who ever walked upon the sea. Still, he was a foreigner—perhaps a Genoese—as was Paulinus of York, as was Theodore of Canterbury. Equally interesting after 1066 is William of Rochester, the baker who set aside every tenth loaf for the poor—an heroic encouragement to all bakers. He was murdered by his own adopted son, it appears; and a chapel was built on the site of the crime, the remains of which can be seen

on the road to Maidstone. This William, however, was a
Scotsman from Perth, as Aidan was an Irishman from Iona.

If these great personages are denied to us through the accident
of birth, there are others again who have been lost to us through
emigration. All of these were venerated for long after their
passing, and some may be venerated still for anything that we
know; but, because they lived and fought the good fight in
foreign countries, their cult has been confined to the places
sanctified by their merits and virtues.

Thus, a number of our countrymen are identified with the
conversion of Sweden, two of whom laid down their lives for the
faith. Again, St. Henrik, the first Bishop of Upsala, was an
Englishman. Blessed Vyevain is honoured at Pontigny in France
and is said to have been Archbishop of York; but there is no trace
of his name in the list of occupants of that see. Well authenticated
however is Blessed William, one of the companions of St. Francis,
who died at Assisi in 1232, six years after the Poor Man himself.
This friar appears in a martyrology under March the second as
" William a priest of Englande." There is another St. William,
also an English emigrant, whose shrine at Pontoise was for long
the resort of pilgrims.

If the laity just manage to come into the picture, the secular
clergy do not come into it at all, not as such. A lively writer
represents the Curé of Ars brooding over a similar phenomenon,
the phenomenon namely that, down to his date, no such French
priest had ever been canonized—" not even a little one."

Everybody now knows how triumphantly the Curé himself was
to retrieve the omission. In the case of this country, the omission
has been more than retrieved by the English Martyrs. Two
hundred and twenty of these were priests, and the majority were
seculars, including one of the very first victims of Henry VIII's
tyranny. Our pastoral clergy can take farther comfort from this,
that the foremost spiritual classic emanating from medieval
England, *The Cloud of Unknowing*, was almost certainly written in
a presbytery by an ordinary parochial incumbent.

Perhaps the root explanation of the shrinkage is to be found in the spirit of caution which began to dominate the Church about this period. In the days of Cuthbert, the calendar was very accessible indeed ; wide was the gate, so that many were they who entered thereat. Then came disciplinary measures calculated to narrow the port of entry. These tended to become tighter and tighter as the centuries passed, as can be gathered if the reader will take the trouble to read the declaration printed on page vii. This affirmation, those who have the hardihood to write books about saints are obliged to make in the interest of law and order. It is this intervention that accounts for much of the falling-off in England after 1066, as the absence of it does for the swollen state of our calendar before that date. Of the thirty-three archbishops who ruled at Canterbury before the Conquest, fourteen bear the title of saint ; but from the Conquest onwards only three are so distinguished. Winchester had six canonized bishops before 1066 but none at all after ; while London has done nothing in that way since St. Dunstan's day. All the saints of the see of Worcester are Anglo-Saxons, and, with the exception of St. John Fisher whom Henry VIII put to death, no bishop of Rochester has been canonized since St. Ithamar, the year of whose consecration is given as 644. He, by the way, was the very first native to be raised to the episcopal dignity. Yet when we come to examine these same lists, we find a considerable number of bishops in the Anglo-Norman period pre-eminent both for learning and virtue, so much so that, had they lived before the Conquest, they must have been raised to the altar by their grateful and edified compatriots. Grossteste, Bishop of Lincoln, is one example, and an example so outstanding that we have placed him among the probable candidates. And there were others besides Grossteste.

Of Guizot, the French statesman, his daughter used to say, " My father is a very good man really ; that he does not always appear so is the result of politics." And there may be something in that, something that partly accounts for the shrinkage that occurred among leading ecclesiastics. With the Conquest, there began to develop a type of bishop which was not exactly a complete novelty, but which was new enough in contrast with the Anglo-Saxon variety. Lanfranc, we know, exerted himself to transfer the episcopal sees from mere villages to bigger centres of population, to make the bishop a city man. This was the Roman tradition and the state of affairs at first in the kingdom of the Franks where the city was the unit of political organization. Amongst the Germans and Celts, however, city life was almost unknown and, consequently, the tribe was the political unit. Hence perhaps the extreme and fascinating simplicity of men like Cuthbert and Aidan, Dunstan and Wulstan and many more. It is true, there was a certain gorgeousness about St. Wilfred, but it did not amount to much after all and was feeble in comparison with that which came in with William the Conqueror.

Then, again, if the Church tended more and more to become dependent on the State, the reverse was also true. The later Roman Empire could count on the services of trained civil servants but these disappeared in time until, eventually, the clerical body alone could provide competent administrators and councillors. In this way, bishops developed into politicians, diplomats and secular judges ; and, by consequence, into territorial princes owning vast estates, levying taxes and copying the pomp and circumstance of temporal rulers. This, under all the circumstances was no doubt inevitable ; but it led to what sometimes looked uncommonly like the secularization of the Church. Anselm, the monk of Bec, on being appointed by William Rufus, clenched his fist so fast that it took half a dozen hefty bystanders all their time to force his hand open for the episcopal staff. Becket's unwillingness is a commonplace of English history, and men like Edmund Rich were very reluctant indeed. But there were some who exhibited no such detachment or squeamishness.

The easy inference would appear to be that the situation of these spiritual potentates made their sanctification a matter of unusual difficulty. But against this facile conclusion we have the notorious fact that a round half dozen of those most deeply involved in State affairs were men of eminent personal sanctity. Twenty-seven and, at one time, twenty-nine English abbots sat in Parliament, as well as two priors—mostly Benedictines. Yet Thomas More sat in Parliament, and it would be asking for trouble to suggest that those who do so need not aspire to the honours of sainthood.

At any rate, in this matter, medieval England was no worse off than the rest of Christendom, no worse off than the seat of Christendom itself. The first fifty-four popes, with one exception, were accorded the title of saint; but after the assumption of the Temporal Power in 755 there is a marked decline, while from 1066 to the present day four only have been so honoured—a tribute surely to papal impartiality.

Anglo-Norman England, therefore, was handicapped by the circumstance that, round about the time of the Conquest, Rome more or less took the responsibility into her own keeping. From then onwards the thing was not to be decided on the spot, first by means of a show of hands and then, decisively, by the mandate of this or that bishop. Custom, of course, died hard and, consequently, we find the people at large still asserting themselves. But in this matter, the *vox populi* does not appear to have been effective to any serious extent.

Waltheof, Earl of Northumberland, was arrested on suspicion of conspiring against the Conqueror, and was executed on a hill overlooking Winchester. By all the disaffected, that is to say by the bulk of the nation, he was not only regarded as a martyr, but was acclaimed such in no uncertain voice. Miracles were reported to have taken place at his tomb in Crowland Abbey, and for many years he was devoutly invoked as St. Waltheof. Meanwhile, at the other extremity of the country, a certain Anglo-Saxon thane called Ligulf was murdered in the night by the servants of the Norman Bishop of Durham. This victim of the transition was likewise " canonized " out of hand by a wave of popular indignation which, eventually, tracked down and assassinated the said bishop for suspected complicity in the crime.

Much later on we have a popular attempt to " canonize " two prelates. Simon of Sudbury, Archbishop of Canterbury, was in 1381 murdered by Wat Tyler's followers, at the very hour when Richard II was negotiating with the rebel leader at Mile End. Although a weak man, he was a peace-loving and amiable one. In consequence, many lamented his death and honoured him as a martyr. His head is supposed to have been sent as a relic to his native town and, indeed, what passes for it is shown to visitors frequenting the magnificent church, overlooking the croft, which stands on the site of the house in which he was born.

Richard le Scrope became primate of the north in the year 1389. He supported the rebellion that broke out against the exactions and tyranny of Richard II who, in the sequel, lost his crown and his life. Richard was succeeded by Henry IV and, in his reign, occurred the revolts of the Percys in which the archbishop was implicated. He was beheaded at York. At the time, and for long after, he was invoked by the northerners as St. Richard the Martyr.

But the veneration accorded to these four was short-lived, and it was never energetic enough to secure for them a place in the English Calendar. Only one instance is there where the local authority and the popular will appear to have effectively by-passed the jurisdiction of the Holy See. In the year 1295, the French made a sort of Commando-raid on Dover in search of plunder. The monks of the Benedictine Priory under the Castle fled as soon as the alarm was given, having first secreted their church plate and other valuables. Unhappily, one venerable old man was left behind in the infirmary and was too helpless to shift for himself. He was found by the raiders and, on refusing to betray the hiding place of the treasure, was callously butchered in his bed. Deplorable though this was, it was hardly sufficient to make a martyr of him. Although his cause was opened in Rome at the request of King Richard II, it was never carried beyond the initial stages. However, the people seem to have taken the thing into their own hands, for an altar dedicated to him existed in Dover priory church as late as the year 1500. He is honoured as St. Thomas of Dover, but he appears to have been a native of Hales in Gloucestershire.

But Anglo-Norman England was farther handicapped by the additional fact that, especially towards the end of the Middle Ages, the Papacy found its hands full of other and more urgent matters. From the fourteenth century onwards, Christendom was afflicted by a succession of calamities almost without precedent in her annals. God, apparently, willed to show the divine origin of His Church by permitting the Evil One to mobilize all his forces against her. Never before had she stood so close to the brink of that precipice down which our Lord promised that she would never fall. Yet this period coincided with the fine flowering of English mysticism in the persons of Juliana of Norwich, Richard Rolle, Walter Hylton, Margery Kempe, and the author of *The Cloud of Unknowing*. The equivalent of this high spirituality is nowhere to be found in Anglo-Saxon times. By those on the spot, these great contemplatives were looked upon as saints, and no efforts were spared to push forward the cause of most of them. The efforts, however, were unavailing, thanks to the tragic confusion of the times.

It would be interesting to know how many canonizations the Holy See carried through during the years made momentous by the Black Death, the Hundred Years War, the Great Schism, and the Babylonian Captivity of the Papacy. That it was difficult to get things done at this time we may well believe ; and it happens that we have downright evidence of the difficulty provided for us by the facts concerning the last English saint to be canonized prior to the Reformation. John of Bridlington died in 1379. In 1386 a mandate was issued to collect evidence in favour of his cause, upon which cause Boniface XI set the seal of his approval by means of a formal Bull. This Bull, however, was never promulgated, and it lay hidden away in the Vatican archives until it was brought to light some fifty years ago, the result being that in the calendars drawn up before this discovery, John's name does not appear at all.

CLOISTER-GARTH

THE monastic style of living was introduced into western Europe from Egypt by way of Rome. It was introduced into this country from Ireland through the agency of the Celtic missionaries, and introduced again in its Benedictine form at the time of the landing of St. Augustine, some sixty years or so after Benedict had written his famous Rule high up in the crisp air of Monte Cassino. In fact, Canterbury can almost certainly claim the distinction of having set up the first Benedictine foundation to be made outside Italy.

In the period of history covered by this book, these religious houses multiplied thick and fast. William of Malmesbury assures us that, in his day, there was not a wealthy man in England but thought shame of himself if he had not contributed to the establishment of a monastery. Medieval writers appear to have taken for granted that society consists of those who work, those who ward, and those who pray. The monks and nuns were the prayers. Certainly this country stood alone amongst the nations of Europe by reason of the number of cathedrals served by these monastics; Canterbury, Durham, Winchester, Rochester, Worcester, Norwich, Ely, Coventry and Bath had Benedictine chaplains. In parenthesis, this England of ours, which owed her conversion to the work of monks, was the first amongst the nations of Europe to make a clean sweep of these same monks, to liquidate her entire monastic system practically at one blow. As an extra aside, we may note, too, that of the fifty or so who were done to death for the Catholic allegiance in the reign of Henry VIII, no fewer than twenty-three were members of religious orders.

But this institution interests us, at the moment, only in so far as it implicates our Anglo-Norman saints. Quite a number of these were professed monastics, while most of the remainder had monastic contacts of various kinds. Thomas Becket began his

3

education at Merton Abbey and, in his troubles, could always count on the hospitality of monks. It was to the shelter of a foreign cloister that Edmund Rich withdrew before the truculence of Henry III. St. Wulstan began as a Benedictine and ended as Bishop of Worcester. As a compensation, his parents began as husband and wife and ended as monk and nun.

The most conspicuous offshoot of the Benedictine body was the Cistercian congregation or group which came into being when William Rufus occupied the throne. This order spread so rapidly throughout Europe that, in less than a hundred years, it was able to count no fewer than fifteen hundred foundations. Although it originated in France, it owed its success and its cohesion in no small degree to the organizing genius of an Englishman. This is Stephen Harding, who has never been properly appreciated by his countrymen, maybe because, like Alcuin, he lived mostly abroad. After leaving Sherborne Abbey school our saint travelled to Scotland, to Paris, and to Rome. Then he tried his hand as a monk in a Benedictine monastery in the diocese of Langres. Things went well for a while, but the community became too large for the taste of the more fervent ones, and so they went off and made a foundation at Citeaux near Dijon. The name Citeaux like that of other foundations that followed later—Fountains, for example, and Sept Fons—suggests water and, in fact, this memorable locality was at first no more than a marshy wilderness. Trees were cut down, and a house built into which the twenty-one moved in 1098—the first Cistercians, Cistercian being from *Cistertium*, the Latin name for Citeaux. Stephen was the third abbot, but he is regarded as part-founder of the order whose members keep his festival with an octave. Besides a directory, he copied out a first-rate version of the scriptures which was to serve as a pattern for all Cistercian bibles. The collection of statutes which he drafted was called the *Charter of Charity*, and a better name for a code of laws has never been invented. Extreme old age left him helpless and half-blind ; and we are told that once, when he was sick unto death and could in nowise stomach the customary fare a bird brought to his cell a cooked fish and fed him therewith, bit by bit, out of its beak.

The first English foundation of this order was at Waverley near Farnham in Surrey. Before long it had a community of nearly two hundred. Fountains, Rievaulx, Beaulieu, Tintern, Furness and Whalley followed, names which to us represent little more than entries in a guide-book for tourists. But Fountains was for many centuries the glory of the North. To-day it is in ruins, ruins of all others in England the largest and most imposing. Some idea of the abbey's grandeur may be gained from the fact that its church was 351 feet long with a nave 65 feet wide, its refectory 108 feet by 45, its cloister 300 feet in length, with a breadth of 42. And Fountains was glorious for better reasons than these. It began well and it ended well. One of its founders was canonized, while the last but one of its thirty-eight abbots— William Thirsk by name—was executed at Tyburn for refusing the Oath of Supremacy.

The co-founder in question is Robert the Cistercian, a York-shireman who became a Benedictine monk after being a secular priest. Leaving York and the Benedictines, he and twelve others journeyed along the banks of the river Skell until they found a suitable site about two and a half miles from Ripon. Here they set up their improvised monastery in the year 1132. Springs abounded in the neighbourhood, and so they called the place Fountains. For a time, they fared so badly that the project was almost abandoned. Plenty of water there was but precious little besides. Then they were joined by three secular priests of the diocese. Their money saved the situation, and building operations were begun. The new community was affiliated to the Cistercian Order by St. Bernard of Clairvaux himself who, curiously enough, was born at Fountains near Dijon. In his letters, he praises the fervour and unworldliness of the Yorkshire foundation where there was neither moroseness nor sadness, strife nor laziness. The inspiration of this religious earnestness was St. Robert. He had the gift of prophecy. He worked miracles.

When new branches began to be formed, he became abbot of Newminster near Morpeth.

Another Cistercian is St. Aelred, who was educated at Hexham, and was later invited to the Scottish court, where he became *major domo*. It proved so wise an appointment that every effort was made to detain him in the kingdom, even after he had made up his mind to follow a higher call and devote himself to the service of a greater Sovereign. At last came the break-away, and it was as complete as he could make it. Returning to Northumberland, he entered the Cistercian order at Rievaulx in Yorkshire. Rievaulx is Valley of the Rie, a small stream near Helmesley. This foundation was in a spot so retired that only the sun and the mist seemed at home there.

Aelred was the third abbot, and under him the house became a brilliant centre of learning and holiness. Great pressure was brought to bear to have him made bishop, but he resisted. One of his monks has left behind some details of his spirit. " For seventeen years," he tells us, " I lived under his rule and during all that time he expelled no one." He found time to visit Scotland twice and to travel as far as Citeaux, the Mother house of his order, which lies four leagues from Dijon. He suffered severely from gout and gall-stones. But this made no difference ; he kept calm and found time for literary work, compiling various biographies, as well as a first-hand account of the battle of the Standard and of the founding of Fountains Abbey. In his youth, he had delighted in the writings of Cicero, and a trace of this attachment can be seen in the title of one of his books, *De Amicitia Spirituali, On Spiritual Friendship*. His humility did not prevent him going in for special preaching—a venture, by the way, as exciting as mountain-climbing, and perhaps as dangerous. We gather that he pronounced the panegyric on St. Edward in Westminster, when the translation of the incorrupt body of the Confessor took place in the presence of King Henry II and Thomas Becket.

It was from Rievaulx that a band of Cistercians set out, in 1136, in order to make the first foundation of their order in

Scotland. By a sort of instinct, they directed their course to a broad glen near the Tweed, two miles distant from the Celtic monastery where St. Cuthbert had lived five centuries before. This was the beginning of Melrose Abbey, as distinct from the aforesaid Abbey of Old Melrose, and it was completed within the short space of ten years, a testimony to the building-energy of the Cistercians, for which they soon became famous.

One of the first abbots of this foundation was St. Walthen or Waltheof, whose mother was the niece of William the Conqueror and the wife of King David of Scotland. Although brought up amid all the luxury of the court, Walthen's vocation began to take shape while he was yet in the nursery. We are told that, whereas his brother amused himself by making paper castles, he made paper churches. He was obliged to take part in the chase, but he took care to separate himself from the rest as soon as possible, when he would dismount, give his bow and arrows to a page, and then retire to some thicket in order to pray. A lady, according to the prevalent custom, sent him a ring which he put on his finger. However, the remark of his companions, " Now Walthen begins to be a lady's man," was the end of the ring. He became a priest soon after, and, then, at the instigation of St. Aelred, a Cistercian. Four years after his profession he was elected abbot of Melrose. During his term of office, the abbey came to be known as the Paradise of the Poor, since the alms that went out from it supported the entire country-side. During the famine of 1154, four thousand hungry people came and settled around Melrose. They remained for a good part of the year. To prevent them from going hungry, Walthen reduced the rations of his monks to one half, sacrificed all the sheep and cattle of the monastery and, when every other expedient failed, miraculously multiplied such scanty provisions as were available. When the last summons came to the abbot, he bade the brethren lift him from his bed and lay him upon the ash-strewn floor, in which Franciscan posture he died at a very great age.

This Walthen was long remembered as the saint who, like

Anthony of Padua, had been favoured by a vision of the divine Child. This happened one morning during the celebration of Mass. It is well known that St. Edmund Rich was similarly favoured. As a young Oxford student, he met the Infant Jesus in person when he was walking across Christ-Church meadows ; and, in memory of what passed between them, he used every night after to mark his forehead with the sign of the cross and say, " Jesus of Nazareth "—a practice which exists among Catholics even at the present day. It was at this time, too, that he made his vow of chastity and, as a pledge thereof, bought two rings, one of which he wore, while placing the other on the finger of the Blessed Virgin's statue.

Akin to Stephen Harding, in many ways, is another monastic saint with whom modern Catholics are well acquainted. This is Simon Stock, the Kent man, who—as we have seen—had a strong partiality for climbing trees and living in them. If we are to believe a reliable tradition, it was to him that the Virgin Mother appeared, promising very special protection to all those who should wear the habit of the Carmelite Order of which, by that time, he himself was a member. Later this promise was taken to extend to those of the laity who might wish to identify themselves with the main body by wearing its scapular or shoulder-piece, this scapular being a strip of cloth some eighteen inches wide and anything up to ten feet long. You slip your head through a hole in the middle and so have several feet of cloth hanging down back and front. In due course, for the convenience of lay people, this garment was reproduced in miniature—a couple of segments of material, three inches by two, connected together by tapes. A generation or so ago, there were few Catholic shirts or shifts that did not harbour one or other of these same segments of cloth. In this way, the faithful could hardly help knowing something about Simon Stock. Popular pictures of the saint show him kneeling before the Blessed Virgin, and receiving from her hand the miniature scapular complete with tapes. Sometimes he is represented in the company of a dog, the same animal no doubt that was accustomed daily to fetch his ration of bread while he was living in his tree.

The Carmelites arrived in England in 1241 and Simon joined them soon after. Three years later, he was made vicar general of the western provinces. Then he spent six years on Mount Carmel and assisted at a Chapter held there. In the end, he became head of the whole body which he governed for twenty years and so successfully that it spread everywhere. At the time of the suppression, the English section had thirty-nine houses.

St. Robert Flower comes upon the scene, in the first instance as an anchorite or solitary, since for years he was the tenant of a cavern hollowed out of the " Rugged rock " which gave its name to the town of Knaresborough in Yorkshire. He belongs to the romantic thirteenth century, and he quitted his hermitage in order to join the romantic Order of Trinitarians.

These Trinitarians were one of several religious bodies vowed to the work of redeeming captives from the hands of the infidels. Most of them died out with the dying out of the evil that brought them into being, but the Trinitarians still survive. In a short time from its founding it had two hundred and fifty houses throughout Christendom. St. Louis of France established one at Fontainebleau, and was accompanied by members of the order on his crusades. The brothers were obliged to set aside one-third of their income as ransom money. The chief source of revenue, apparently, were the box-office receipts derived from the theatrical performances of which they were the promoters. The actors went all over Europe preceded by trumpeters and cymbal-players who served as publicity-agents. In due course, a stage would be erected and a drama acted illustrating the misfortunes of Christians in Mussulman hands. In this way hearts were touched and purses opened. Later on, flag days were organized on a gigantic scale. A veritable army of collectors was enrolled authorized by letters-patent to visit this or that town. As soon as the empty chests were filled, three or four of the brothers would set sail for Tunis or Algiers.

In this daring enterprise many lost their lives. Moreover
they were always liable to lose their freedom, since, if the sum
they brought did not satisfy the cupidity of the infidels, the
friars were promptly clapped in gaol until the arrival of fresh
funds. One, St. Serapion, an Englishman, actually offered himsel
in ransom. Eighty-seven captives were exchanged for him at
Algiers. In his new quarters, he converted so many Moors that
he was crucified in the year 1240. The number redeemed during
three centuries is estimated at 90,000, among them Cervantes, the
author of the immortal Don Quixote. He was, in fact, buried
among the Trinitarians at Madrid, and in the habit of their order
which was a combination of red, white and blue.

But perhaps the most remarkable of all these medieval monastery men is St. Gilbert of Sempringham, for he has the unique
distinction of being the only Englishman who ever founded a
religious order in the complete sense. Moreover, what Gilbert
planned and brought into being was a monastic establishment
that was English to the core, owing allegiance to no foreign
superior whatsoever, the Pope excepted. It was a double order
besides, that is to say, one in which men and women were housed
more or less together, an experiment familiar enough to the
Anglo-Saxons but extremely rare in medieval times.

It is comforting to learn that Gilbert began badly. Apparently
he was a very sickly child, as well as a naughty one ; just the sort
of urchin over whom certain pundits are fond of pronouncing
woeful prophecies. The servants, taking their cue from the
father who had an unnatural dislike for his son, made game of
him from morning to night, so that the puzzled youth grew
sullen and morose. Books frightened him, and he would not
learn. God knows how such a child might have turned out had
it not been for his mother. As it was, he grew up to be an
organizing genius of the first order, with a fund of patience and
a deep understanding of human nature. There was no moroseness
about him in after life ; just the reverse, for we are told that once
when he and his supporters were waiting outside the law-court

for their case to come on, he bought some mechanical toys from a street vendor and amused the company with them until their names were called.

He was already a priest when he inherited his father's property, and this enabled him to realize what used to be described as the darling ambition of every French curé. He gave a rule of life to seven young women and built a convent for them adjoining his church. All went well and, presently, he instituted some lay serving brothers to manage the farm and fields. Eventually, a community of canons was established to act as chaplains. The founder lived to see thirteen convents in working order. The sisters were dressed in white, and in winter wore a tippet of sheepskin and a black cap lined with wool. From time to time, there was trouble with the lay brothers, who were mostly uncouth rustics recruited from the serfs of the neighbourhood. But the order was popular, and received great favour from the Crown. One of Gilbert's rules was that all the animals found in the domains of his monasteries were to be treated with consideration, another that no beggar was to be turned from the door unbefriended. He lived to be one hundred and six, so that he is the patriarch of our collection ; altogether an attractive character, and a practical man to boot, for he compiled a handbook for the benefit of architects concerned with the building of religious houses.

A PEARL AMONG WOMEN

THE chief authority for St. Margaret's *Life* is a contemporary memoir abounding in details; so much so, indeed, that it is thought to have been the work of her confessor, Turgot, a monk of Durham, who later became Archbishop of St. Andrews. We have, besides, a panegyric attributed to St. Aelred who, as we have seen, belonged for a time to the household of Margaret's son David, regarded as one of the best rulers that Scotland ever had. Aelred, therefore, had access to reports and traditions that were still very much alive. Thanks to these two, the saint really comes to life before our eyes. What makes Turgot's chronicle so attractive is the circumstance that it was written for and at the request of the saint's own daughter Maud. The monk keeps this circumstance steadily in mind all through, and is careful to record those homely fireside details which appeal to the feminine curiosity. At the same time, he steers clear of the temptation which naturally besets an artist commissioned to paint a family portrait. " I suppress many things," he says, " that redound to your mother's honour, lest I may be suspected of trying to flatter your queenly dignity." About Margaret's miracles he is very reticent indeed. " Others may admire the indications of sanctity which they afford; I admire much more the works of mercy which she performed."

We may mention here that this same daughter, the wife of our own Henry I, was herself canonized after a fashion, so that if there was one black sheep amongst Margaret's children—and this fact may console all good Christian mothers in like case—there was a saint as well. Maud or Matilda was looked up to by the whole nation and, in particular, by the Londoners for whom she built a hospital at St. Giles, a priory within Aldgate and a bridge over the Lea at Stratford. Altogether, she so successfully emulated her mother's example that she was enrolled in the calendar and her feast kept on the twentieth of April. She lies in Westminster

Abbey near the tomb of Edward the Confessor, but her unofficial cult does not appear to have been perpetuated.

For all his objectivity, Turgot's enthusiasm is manifest on every page. " She was called Margaret," he says, " and in God's sight she did indeed prove to be a Pearl precious in faith and in good deeds. She put out her hand to strong things." He does complete justice to her woman's instinctive love of smart clothes. She always dressed well, it appears ; and she made Malcolm dress well, a thing he was not accustomed to do until she became his wife. But having paid this tribute to her human nature, Turgot assures us that all the time she was at heart poorer than any of the paupers whom she befriended. And though she had a tenderness for poverty she had none at all for dirt, seeing no reason why the two should go hand-in-hand in a place like Scotland, where water was so pure and so abundant. Elsewhere our biographer compares her to Esther. Esther's family, like Margaret's, was the victim of political tyranny and each woman was born in exile ; it was love-at-first-sight that made each the consort of a king, and each used all the influence of her position in favour of the needy and the oppressed.

At his very first interview with Margaret, Malcolm " cast such love unto her that there and then he prevailed upon her to become his wife ; and thereafter her sunny face, her witty speech, and her every movement were delightful to him. From her he learned to watch in prayer often throughout the entire night, and it amazed me (Turgot) to see such fervour and devoutness in a secular man. Plainly seeing that Christ dwelt in the heart of his queen he was always willing to take her advice in works of justice, mercy and almsgiving." There can be few in Scotland unacquainted with the story of how the King, being unable to read, was accustomed to kiss the books that lay in his wife's apartment. One of these may well have been her copy of the Gospels, richly adorned with jewels, which is now in the Bodleian library at Oxford.

And there can be few in Scotland unacquainted with the episode that gave rise to the proverb ' *Gin the Buckle Bide*.' It seems that, when the Queen went abroad, she rode behind a chamberlain whose responsibility it was to bring her safely over moor and fen and running stream. There was one river, however, that really proved too much for the chamberlain. It was in spate to such a degree that he had to fasten Margaret's belt to his own buckle, which meant that she was safe as long as he was safe, and no longer. In the deepest part, the horse began to flounder. " Grip hard," cried the chamberlain, " we'll win owre yet." " Ay," the Queen replied, " we'll win owre, gin the buckle bide." The buckle did bide and, as a reward for his service, the chamberlain was authorized to adorn his shield with buckles, and to take for the motto of his family the words *Grip Hard*. This family later became an important Scottish house, and the Leslie shield still bears its band of buckles and its proud reminder to *Grip Hard*.

It is clear from what Turgot tells us that this bustling mother of a large family, burdened with so many responsibilities and anxieties, contrived to reach a high degree of contemplation and of union with God. " She lived always in the divine presence and her life was a continual prayer." In Lent she recited the entire psalter three or four times a day.

> The Queen,
> Oftener on her knees than on her feet,
> Died every day she lived.

This is what Shakespeare says, in *Macbeth*, of Malcolm's mother ; but, as an anonymous writer points out, it was really of Malcolm's wife that he was thinking when he wrote the words. " Only her body was here below, for her spirit was elsewhere." She generally heard all the Masses that were said in the royal chapel, being still at her devotions when the household assembled for the High Mass.

St. Margaret has been blamed for having altered the official language of her adopted country from Gaelic to Saxon or Broad Scots. She herself never learned to speak Gaelic well ; and, although the majority of the people continued to use it for long after her death, the court never returned to it again. However, it is just possible that this change-over was coming along in any case. She had too much respect and veneration for Columba ever to have hated the tongue in which he preached ; and, if she discouraged it in those about her, this was an unfortunate by-product of the tidying-up process which she felt it her duty to initiate. She found everything in the royal entourage rather uncouth and lacking in refinement. The general taste was backward. Malcolm himself was a rough and ready lump of a man whose manners—even table manners—she set herself to improve. She made him conduct himself as became his dignity. She introduced the " Grace Cup " into his banquets. It seems that, before her time, when the meal was ended the guests were accustomed to stampede, leaving the chaplain to get on with the prayers. To stop this, she announced that, in future, after Grace had been said, a cup of the best wine would be provided for each guest from her own table, which wine she wished to be drunk in her own honour. For centuries after, this Grace Cup followed every Scottish feast, and it became a strict point of etiquette to partake of it.

She had rich tapestries made for the royal apartments and, rare thing in the Scotland of that date, panes of glass which were carried from Dunfermline to Edinburgh, and *vice versa*, according to the movement of the court. Malcolm was the first Scottish king to use Edinburgh Castle as a residence, and credit for this choice is usually assigned to the influence of his Queen. The church which she caused to be built at Dunfermline was the largest and fairest thing of its kind in the whole country. When the Western Isles fell into Malcolm's hands in 1072, she rebuilt the monastery and church at Iona, and provided an endowment for the monks whom she brought in. Workshops of all kinds she established, inviting skilled craftsmen from the Continent to teach her own subjects how to fashion things of taste and beauty. " There was no need," writes Freeman the historian, " for this woman to bring a new religion into Scotland, but she did give a new life to the religion which she found existing there."

For years before her, St. Andrews had been the ecclesiastical centre of Scotland, and a popular place of pilgrimage. For these the Queen built hostels on either shore of the Forth, the sites of which are now covered by the villages of North and South Queensferry. At her own expense, she provided servants to wait on the pilgrims and ships to carry them across the estuary. For all his virtues, Malcolm her husband was fond of fighting; much too fond, indeed. She, apparently, could not stop these battles and expeditions, but one of her favourite charities was to provide for the numerous orphans resulting therefrom. Slavery was the greatest social curse of eleventh-century Scotland, and here again the Queen's influence could go no further than alleviations. She spent large sums of money in ransoming the prisoners of war who automatically became the slaves of their captors, and she employed agents to bring her news of any exceptionally hard cases.

As to the administration of justice, she found that in a very unsatisfactory condition. Wrongs were numerous and redress lay, for the most part, only in a petition to the King, who was almost sure to be miles away with his army. Margaret became Sheriff, Lord Advocate and Public Prosecutor all in one. Like St. Wulstan, she spent several hours of the day listening to grievances. She next appointed as detectives men on whom she could rely, whose duty it was to move about the land and keep their eyes and ears wide open. They then made their report, and she acted. This measure was so successful that, when her son David came to the throne, he turned these detectives into itinerary judges authorized to act everywhere in the King's name.

Margaret enters upon the scene surrounded by misfortunes, and she quits it to the very same accompaniments. Malcolm met his death in battle with William Rufus. According to the Scottish historians, he was besieging the castle of Alnwick at the time, and the English garrison, offering to surrender, desired the King to come up and receive the keys with his own hand. He did come up, but the soldier who made the presentation thrust the spear carrying the keys into Malcolm's eye, and killed him. This account has been questioned. What is certain is that Malcolm did perish in this war, together with his son Edward. At the very same hour, far away in Edinburgh, the Queen suddenly said to those about her : " It may be that this day a greater evil hath befallen Scotland than any this long time." She did not long survive.

" She had," Turgot tells us, " a foresight of her death before it happened ; for, speaking to me of certain matters, at the end she said : ' Farewell ! because I shall not be here much longer ; and you will stay behind me only for some little time. Two requests I have to make ; and one is, that so long as you live, you will remember my poor soul in your Masses and prayers, and the other, that you stand by my children and teach them to fear and love God.' When her end drew near, she rose from her bed and went into her oratory to receive the Viaticum. Then, feeling a fever upon herself, she went back to bed, and desired her chaplains to recite the psalms to her and recommend her soul to the divine mercy. In the meantime, she called for the Black Cross, embraced it and signed herself frequently with it and recited the *Miserere*. When she had made an end, her son Edgar coming in from the army, she asked him how his father and brother did. He fearing to alarm her, said they were well. She answered him : ' I know how it is.' Then lifting up her hands to heaven, she praised God saying : ' I thank Thee that in sending so great an affliction in the last hour of my life, Thou would'st purify me from my sins, as I hope, by Thy mercy.' Before long, finding her last moments approach, she repeated from the prayers of the Church for that occasion the following aspiration : ' O Lord Jesus Christ, who by Thy death hast given life to the world, deliver me from all evil.' Praying thus, she was loosed from the bonds of her mortal body on the sixteenth of November 1093, in the fifty-seventh year of her age."

For centuries after, the bedroom was left just as it was when she expired, and even in the days of the early Stuarts it was still known as *The Blessed Margaret's Chamber*. The memory of what she had been and had done produced a veritable crop of legends, particularly throughout Fife and the Edinburgh district. Whatever may be the historical value of this folk-lore, it does testify to the completeness with which she had lived in the hearts of her people. Even to-day, up there in the north, the name Margaret is a general favourite. If her own countrymen displayed no great enthusiasm for her cult, this is probably explained by the fact that she was the wife of a king who, for years, harried the English border without stint or mercy.

Two fountains in Edinburgh bear her name, one being in the gardens near the castle, and the other in the King's Park south of Holyrood Palace. Near this second well is a sheet of clear water called St. Margaret's Loch. The land-locked bay on the western side of the Forth Bridge, now the naval base of Rosyth, is still known as St. Margaret's Hope, the tradition being that it was on its strand that the saint's foot rested for the first time on Scottish soil. On her journeys between Dunfermline and Edinburgh she crossed the river at points where the extremities of the Forth Bridge now stand, which points still retain the names of North and South Queensferry. Midway between the capital and the latter village there lies the fragment of a dolmen or cromlech upon which she is supposed to have rested, and this is known as St. Margaret's Stone. Finally, at Dunfermline itself, St. Margaret's Cave is still intact, a gloomy cavern to which she often retired to pray, a practice which led to the only misunderstanding that ever existed in her married life.

In the Anglo-Norman calendar, St. Margaret appears as the sole representative of the laity strictly so called, and she is the only English woman who has been canonized since the Conquest. This circumstance might seem to challenge the inclusiveness and co-ordinating power of the Christian faith, as though it had no very great sanctifying influence over life as the masses have to live it, as God wills that they should live it. It is the sort of challenge implicit in some of the medieval works of art, portraitures of heaven as an ecclesiastical reservation peopled by church dignitaries, the men tonsured and the women clad in conventual garments. Regrettable though this may be, it in nowise represents the authentic Christian viewpoint. It has never been suggested that those who would unite themselves to God and fulfil Christ's ideal, must of necessity choose the path that leads either to the sacristy or to the cloister. There is only one fundamental holiness, namely the holiness of the Christian. All are members of the mystical body, although the members have not the same function. All are, by baptism, made partakers of the divine nature. And if the Church seems to concentrate upon the glorification of clerics this may be to encourage all clerics whose sanctification is, after all, so vital to the cause of religion. So, too, with the monastic ideal. If this be emphasized, then the emphasis is of service to the world which requires, and will always require, to be reminded that the things it so ardently covets can be fertile sources of spiritual and moral danger. But, as a matter of fact, no English nun has been canonized since Anglo-Saxon times, and not a single nun figures in the list of the English Martyrs.

FEUDS AND FRICTIONS

ALL of these are overshadowed by the one that culminated in the murder in the cathedral. But against the theory of those who contend that this famous quarrel was provoked by the inferiority-complex of Becket the man, or by the pugnacity of Becket the Englishman, we have the plain fact that his case was of a piece with dozens of others involving meek and mild prelates, some of whom were not Englishmen at all.

Of St. Anselm, another Archbishop of Canterbury, the historian Freeman says that, although a foreigner, he has won his place amongst the noblest worthies of our realm. And Anselm's tenure of office was a tissue of disputes and vexations with only two peaceful years tacked on at the end. Hugh of Lincoln fared better but not much better. The very sound of his name worked Richard I into a fit of rage.

St. Edmund Rich, the primate, who preached peace in season and out, had no option but to go into exile, where he died. Henry III, whether greedy for money or in need of it, was keeping bishoprics and all manner of benefices vacant in order that their revenues might be diverted to his own purse. This the archbishop thought intolerable, and he said so. It was this same monarch who withheld from St. Richard of Chichester the temporalities of his see so that he had to live on alms like any other beggar. When the see of Chichester fell vacant, Henry nominated a worthless man whose sole merit in the king's eyes lay in his having enriched the royal treasury by out-and-out robbery. Canterbury, however, refused to confirm the election, and chose Richard instead. Henry was furious. The matter went before the Pope, who not only confirmed Richard in his appointment but consecrated him himself. The King thereupon played the cheap and petty tyrant in real earnest. He cut off all supplies, and forbade any subject of his to give the new bishop either money, food or lodging. Had it not been for one courageous priest of Chichester who opened his door to the outcast, Richard might have had to wander about his diocese like a vagabond. For two whole years this state of affairs continued until the Pope threatened Henry with excommunication. At that time—fortunately for liberty, on the whole—such a threat was serious, and the King's backers gave in. Even St. Thomas of Hereford, *inter omnes mitis*, hauled into court and tried without compunction all who threatened the rights of his church, the King's son-in-law amongst them and Llewellyn, Prince of Wales.

In the midst of these chronic contentions, the battle-cry that rose from the ecclesiastical ranks was ever *The Rights of Our Order*. We who live in a totally different age, and have grown accustomed to the separation of Church and State, may have our own opinion as to the validity of some of these rights. But insistence upon them by the prelates concerned was a matter of obvious and conscientious duty. When the Speaker of the House of Commons is elected, the first thing he does is to lay claim to all the rights and privileges of the Commons, let us say of his order. Although we may question the worth of some of these rights and privileges, we do not blame the Speaker; he can do no other if he is to take office at all. And Becket, Edmund, Richard and company were in like case.

This, however, is not to suggest that they were inspired by mere greed or love of power. Such a view of the situation would be cheap and childish in the extreme. This or that pettiness apart, there was solid enough substance in the quarrels. Indeed, the abuse which caused more uproar than any was one that resulted in great hardship to the poor. This was the seizing by the King of vacant bishoprics and benefices in order to swell the royal exchequer. In such cases, the ecclesiastical estates were farmed out to the highest bidder who, of course, exploited his leasehold to his own profit. Under this system of sub-letting, the tenants were ground to the earth by merciless exactions.

Whatsoever their class-interests may have led them to do or

say, these churchmen and the clerical body generally existed as a mediating authority between the strong and the weak; and to their credit it must be said that, on the whole, they fully comprehended and performed the duties of this noble position. To none but themselves would it have been permitted to reprimand the vices of kings and to mitigate the severities of the law. When the decorations of St. Mark's, Venice, were taken in hand, the ruler of the city was kept in mind by the Church. Over one of the altars he could read these words graven in letters of gold: " O Doge! love justice, render to all men their due. May the poor and the widow, the orphan and the ward trust to you as their defender. Let neither fear nor hate, passion nor gold cause you to waver." In those ages, when political power was so liable to abuse, what voice was there besides the voice of religion strong enough and brave enough to utter such warnings? St. Wulstan uttered them in a voice that sounded like a clap of thunder. So we are told. He set up a kind of Citizens' Advice Bureau in the porch of his cathedral, in which he sat each Sunday listening to tales of oppression and injustice. If the complaints were shown to be well-founded, then that day there would be thunder over Worcester and no mistake.

In the meantime, there were frictions enough and to spare within the bosom of the ecclesiastical family itself. For six solid years Grosseteste fought his dean and chapter, and for six solid years dean and chapter fought him. It was a monk who called him a persecutor of monks; but, as an offset, he was actually excommunicated by the Benedictines of Canterbury. St. Edmund Rich, too, was strenuously opposed by the staff of his own cathedral and by the clergy generally. Reformer though he was, the ground was sometimes cut from under his feet by those who appealed to Rome over his head. In the finish, he stood *solitarius in deserto*, alone in a wilderness of friction and misunderstanding.

Thomas of Hereford actually died while under sentence of excommunication—the primate's excommunication, of course. It made no difference to his canonization, however. St. Richard of Chichester's episcopate lasted eight years during which, like his master St. Edmund, he laboured incessantly to raise the moral tone of the clergy. He was not exactly popular with these, although he quite won the hearts of the laity. Towards certain transgressors he showed no mercy, even when the intercession of the primate and the King was on their side. He drew up statutes regulating clerical life in great detail, and obliged each priest to make, or have made, a copy of the same. While he was in charge of the diocese, no relation of his who chanced to be in Holy Orders had the ghost of a chance of promotion, so deep-rooted was his aversion to nepotism. Ingeniously enough, he would instance the example of our Lord Himself who gave the keys, not to His cousin John, but to Peter a blank stranger.

In order to enforce his liturgy upon the Saxon monks of Glastonbury, Thurston, their Norman abbot, entered the church with a band of archers and spearmen. The monks resisted, and a conflict commenced round the altar and behind the great crucifix which was soon stuck thick with arrows, while benches and candelabra were used as weapons by the brethren, several of whom were slain. It was this incident that suggested the necessity for an authoritative order of public prayer which St. Osmund compiled. This was the Sarum Use which may be said to have had a baptism of blood.

When Gilbert of Sempringham was an old man of eighty, he and some of his own subjects were involved in an acrimonious dispute which lasted for years. The start of the thing is thus described by Gilbert himself. "The ring-leaders were two brothers to whom I had entrusted the care of all the houses. One of them I received when he was almost a beggar, the other, Ogger the smith, I admitted before he was a smith, together with his poverty-stricken parents and two sisters, the latter being chronic invalids. These rose up against me and against our rules. God knows how they lied and what evil reports they spread abroad." But the two brothers in question did more. They helped themselves to the goods of the order and, having " grown rich with plunder," set out for Rome to state their case. That His Holiness received them with kindness speaks well for the impartiality of that much-harassed and much-criticized tribunal. In fact, the decision was given in their favour, and poor Gilbert was told to take them back, which he did. This victory, naturally, turned the heads of the other lay-brothers. All the petty grievances, real or imagined, that had simmered for years now bubbled up and over. And the worst of it was that Becket, whom the Gilbertines had befriended at their grievous peril, sided with the rebels and reprimanded the founder severely. In the end, the whole nation was agitated by the quarrel, so that the King had to intervene. And then, by degrees, the misunderstanding was straightened out. Rome reversed her decision. The malcontents submitted, all but the redoubtable Ogger, who went to the dogs altogether and, no doubt, made a bad end. The chronicle calls him " the hammer of Gilbert," an appropriate enough name for a blacksmith.

However, the most disedifying quarrel of all revolves round the person of St. William the primate of the north. From start to finish it is a sordid story ; but it would take a worse to detract from the immense glory that was York. This see has given to Christendom eight saints, to Rome three cardinals, to England twelve Lord Chancellors and two Lord Treasurers, and to the north two Lord Presidents. In Catholic days, the diocese contained 541 parishes. Its religious houses, one hundred and fourteen in all, included some of the largest and most famous in the whole country.

Yet, to the saint in question, the name York was destined to become like so much gall and wormwood, for he became the storm-centre of one of those regrettable disputes concerning the appointment of bishops which for long were very characteristic of the northern see. Some would say that this was the legacy bequeathed to it by Wilfred. At any rate, on consulting its roll of prelates, we find quite a series of appointments and depositions ; and, we may add, a goodly number of ominous vacancies lasting, in some cases, for several years. Even the mutual relations of Canterbury and York were embittered by a protracted struggle for precedence.

William was a Fitzherbert and, tradition says, a nephew of King Stephen. At the instance of his royal uncle, he was elected Archbishop of York after being the treasurer of the cathedral. But there was another candidate in the field, a certain Cistercian monk. What with one thing and another, Canterbury would not consecrate Stephen's nominee pending an appeal to Rome. Then, St. Bernard of Clairvaux, the preacher of the Crusade and himself a Cistercian, threw his weight into the scale in favour of the monastic candidate. But the Pope of Rome could be independent as well, and he decided that William was to remain provided he could clear himself of certain base charges. This, the latter, saintly man that he was, was easily able to do; and so the papal legate consecrated him at Winchester.

This was by no means the end of the matter, although, as far as the city of York was concerned, William's obvious goodness of heart went a long way in the direction of conciliation. But death intervened and caused trouble. A new pope was given to the Church. He was a Cistercian and thus, perhaps, easily got at by the partisans of William's rival. He, poor man, now proposed to set out for Rome in order to receive the pallium, that little circular band or necklace without which an archbishop may not exercise any of his functions. It was not a costly garment, but it was taxed and, besides, there were the expenses of the long journey which William, apparently, had no money to meet. To raise the fare he pawned or sold certain treasures and privileges belonging to his cathedral. It was sheer simplicity on his part, we may be sure; but then this same beautiful simplicity sometimes gets us into trouble. It got him into serious trouble. His enemies represented him as the robber of his diocese, and the Pope suspended him from his functions.

William took refuge with his friend the King of Sicily; but, in the meantime, his other friends in the north did his cause a grave disservice by attacking and destroying Fountains Abbey of which the rival candidate was prior. Our saint bewailed this outrage and did penance for it, for the Sovereign Pontiff promptly deposed him and consecrated the prior of Fountains in his stead. There was nothing for it now but to pray, lie low and wait. This William did at Winchester until such time as His Holiness, St. Bernard and the " intruder " archbishop were no more. And they all died about the same time, strangely enough, namely in 1153. The new pontiff was at once appealed to, and not in vain. William returned to York, pallium and all, and travelling fast came within sight of the minster towers, only to find the road blocked by the dean of the chapter and the archdeacon, who peremptorily forbade him to enter either the city or the diocese. The new archbishop bowed and went forward on his way relying, it appears, on the loyalty and good manners of the ordinary lay people. He was not deceived either, for there was such a crush to see him that a bridge gave way under the strain and many persons fell into the river.

Arrived in his palace, William at once manifested the greatest friendship towards the Cistercians, promising to rebuild their ruined abbey of Fountains. But it was not to be. He survived only a few weeks, and it was hinted—falsely enough—that the clergy had put poison in his chalice.

If we refer in this place to the persecution of the Jews, it is because the repressive measures directed against that long-suffering race, directly or indirectly implicate certain of our medieval saints. Amongst these latter are three youths, venerated as martyrs, whom misguided popular opinion regarded as victims of ritual-murder. The most notorious of these is William of Norwich, a lad of twelve, the date of whose death is given as 1144. The story ran that, on Holy Saturday of that year, a boy's corpse was found outside the city wall. It showed signs of violence, and was not touched until Easter Monday, when it was buried where it was discovered. However, owing to the peculiar nature of the wounds, the Jews were suspected. An episcopal court was, therefore, set up and some evidence taken. The upshot was that the Jews of Norwich were invited to disprove the accusation by submitting themselves to the Ordeal of Fire. Nothing came of this, and the matter was dropped until some years after when a prominent Jew was assassinated. On his relations demanding justice against the assassins, the bishop brought forward the murder of the boy William as a counter-charge.

Our sole authority for the unsavoury tale is a certain monk of Monmouth, a writer of unbounded credulity to say the least. According to him, William was decoyed into a Jewish house and there, after a service in the synagogue, crowned with thorns and crucified. And this foul deed was done " because the Jewish law ordained that annually they must sacrifice a Christian somewhere " ; in the year 1144, the lot had fallen on the Jews of Norwich. Whether he believed this or not, the monk who wrote it down has a deal to answer for. His narration has been well and properly described as " one of the most notable and disastrous lies in history." Disastrous it surely was, for it served as the foundation of the ritual-murder accusation which has been believed from that day to this. The Jewish Encyclopedia gives over one hundred alleged cases going right up to the year 1900. We can only be thankful that our popes have again and again condemned those who make this preposterous accusation, and no single pope has ever lent it the sanction of his name and authority. Alban Butler, who certainly thought that these boys had met their death at the hands of the Jews, describes as slanderous the inference that that race makes or made a ritual practice of such crimes.

The case of St. Hugh of Lincoln belongs to the thirteenth century, and created so deep an impression that it became the subject of popular ballads. Chaucer used it as one of his *Tales* ; while, until quite recently, a pathetic song about the lad's fate was sung in certain parts of the country. Hugh, we are told, was nine years old when he was decoyed into a Jewish house, tortured and crucified. When they tried to bury the remains, the earth threw them up. At any rate, the secret leaked out and the ring-leaders were arrested. By order of Henry III and his parliament, the culprit-in-chief was dragged to death at the heels of a young horse, and eighteen others were hanged at Lincoln. The remaining seventy-three were released through the intervention of the Franciscan or Dominican friars who were accused of having been bribed to interfere by the wealth of Jewry. Hugh's body was interred next to that of Robert Grosseteste. St. Harold of Gloucester was another youth said to have been martyred in this fashion about the year 1168.

To what extent these unfounded accusations influenced the policy of the Crown with respect to English Jewry it is impossible to say. The opening years of Edward I's reign, in particular, were marked by severities which interest us here only in so far as they were associated with St. Thomas Cantelupe, Bishop of Hereford. As a member of the Privy Council, it was his duty to watch over the welfare of the realm. Rightly or wrongly he considered that the Jews, by reason of their usuries, extortions and coining, were a menace to the nation; and so he concurred in the measures taken against them by the sovereign. Some authorities have maintained that he it was who procured their banishment, but all the evidence points to the conclusion that this was, from first to last, the work of the King himself, who was instigated thereto by pecuniary embarrassment. Besides, the proclamation commanding the Jews to go forth from the kingdom was made in 1290, and by that time St. Thomas had been in his grave for eight years.

SERVICES RENDERED

ALL sorts of these there were, direct and indirect, helping in one way or another to ease the burden of other people's lives.

And almsgiving, of course. That goes without saying. This may not be to the taste of those who are inclined to view the ancient charities as a plausible substitute for justice denied. But Christ our Lord knew the wrongs of the poor better than we can know them, and He placed these same old-fashioned benefactions in the very forefront of His precepts—cups of cold water for the thirsty, clothing for the naked, bread for the hungry, and so on. If these saints, then, went astray through defective sociological insight, they went astray in good company.

Nor did it occur to them that they were degrading those to whom they ministered, any more than it occurs to us when we contribute our mite, say to the Red Cross. A condition of indebtedness need not be a degradation, otherwise we are all degraded. We are debtors to those who manufacture our suits and shoes, to cooks and providers, and to none more so than to those who cater for our intellectual and cultural wants. Indeed, the medievalists—taking their cue from the Fathers of the Church—worked out a theory to the effect that almsgiving was really a payment made for services rendered, just as are our rates and doctors' fees and such like. They fancied that God was willing to forgive the world much for the sake of the poor people living in it, and so they maintained that these latter are the creditors of all the others.

Some of these saintly dignitaries, in spite of the positions they held, contrived to live like poor men. Others had no option, as we have seen. Richard of Chichester was forced to beg, as also Stephen Harding and his first associates at Citeaux. At one time, the Carmelites of Oxford were obliged to sell the church pews in order to buy a few loaves of bread. By such behaviour, these people were conferring a distinction upon poverty, the most despised as it is the most universal of human conditions, demonstrating that in such a state may be found peace, dignity and happiness. They made much, too, of intimate and personal services, as against those that are delegated from a safe distance. Hence the interminable washing of feet and serving at table. The youths whom St. Wulstan trained at Worcester were taught to wait upon the poor as part of their education. In such ways, they endeavoured to establish another truce of God in the chronic struggle between those who have too much and those who have too little.

At any rate, through their histories runs the well-worn theme. The first thing Becket did on becoming primate was to double the allowance set aside by his predecessors in favour of those in want, a practice which appears to have been a point of honour among bishops generally. St. John Fisher succeeded to the meanest and smallest diocese in England, for Rochester in his time consisted of ninety-nine West Kent parishes. Hence his remark that he would not exchange his poor old wife for the richest widow in England. But, on taking possession, he divided his meagre revenue into three portions : one for the repair and upkeep of his cathedral, another for the needy and the maintenance of poor scholars, a third for household expenses and the purchase of books. He never tired of visiting the sick in their stifling, smoky hovels, climbing up ladders where stairs were lacking, to sit for hours by the bedside of some sufferer to whom he would give both spiritual and material succour and, if necessary, prepare for death. He distributed food and money daily at his own gate, presiding in person to ensure strict justice. His first biographer described him as " a physician to the ailing, a staff to the lame, the tutor of the orphan and the host of the hungry traveller."

When St. Edmund became treasurer of Salisbury Cathedral, he gave away the bulk of his salary and, in consequence, was poor for the greater part of the year. As preacher of the Crusade, he was entitled and authorized to receive certain fees, but he would not touch a penny—all professional preachers please note. Every farthing he could lay hands on seems to have gone towards the relief of poverty. The young women of his archdiocese were lucky girls, for he had a particular care to provide marriage portions for them. He fought bribery in civil relations and simony in ecclesiastical.

Richard of Chichester was another of the same sort. Capgrave tells us that, on one occasion, a single loaf which the saint blessed sufficed for the needs of three thousand persons; in fact, there was some of the bread left over. The poor got most of the bishop's earnings, and he ministered to them in person to the extent of burying their dead. When his steward complained that the income from all sources was inadequate to meet these charitable demands, he was told to sell off the household plate as well as the bishop's horse. When a fire burnt down some of his property, he regarded the accident as a rebuke to his own covetousness, and so gave things away harder than ever. Providentially enough, he died in a kind of alms-house, that is to say, in the *Maison Dieu*, a dwelling built at Dover for poor priests and pilgrims.

Wulstan, we are informed, celebrated the Maundy for the last time by washing the feet and clothes of the needy, bestowing alms and ministering the cup of charity. On Easter day, he made high festival with his beloved poor. Taking to his bed at length, in the eighty-seventh year of his age, he lay propped up in sight of the altar, and only ceased his service of praise and thanksgiving with the drawing of his last breath.

St. Margaret, Queen of Scotland, never stirred abroad without being besieged by a crowd of widows, orphans and indigent persons whose wants she relieved. She did great work, too, for prisoners of war, generally ransoming them out of her own purse and, of course, without telling her husband, who naturally wondered where all the money was going to—not an unusual experience for husbands the world over. Every morning, on her knees, she fed nine orphans with a breakfast which she cooked herself. During Lent and Advent, as many as three hundred poor people would be brought in, and she and her husband would wait upon them, serving up the same dishes used at the royal table. Hospitals she caused to be built and hospitals she visited. Her services to her adopted country are well known. We are told that, after her own sanctification, the cause that lay nearest to her heart was the happiness of her subjects. She exerted herself to provide them with good priests and good magistrates. She brought culture and refinement in her train, and did more than any to polish the nation, a polishing not always or altogether quite to its taste. There is reason to believe that from her the Scots learned their respect for the Sabbath Day, a lesson which they later took too much to heart. St. Margaret also founded schools, and made it possible for poor children to enter them.

This latter social service was one particularly favoured by our Anglo-Norman saints generally. Soon after our " illiterate " friend St. Wulstan was laid in his grave, popular educational establishments began to spring up all over the land, of which they were eager founders and supporters. Edmund Rich, Thomas of Hereford, Richard le Scrope and Richard Wyche were the indefatigable champions of free education. To Henry VI England owed many scholastic establishments, including Eton and King's College, Cambridge. It was compassion for the ignorance of the common people that induced Gilbert of Sempringham to found his order which, in fact, began as an ordinary free-school. In his day, there were few nunneries in England, and those that did exist were mostly for the well-to-do. His subjects, however, were recruited from the humblest classes. Thanks to him, many of these peasants became proficient Latin scholars. Probably no religious order in England was more popular in the literal and best sense of the word. The Crown regarded it as a national asset, and showed it great favour. Liberal charters were granted by Henry II and his successors. Henry VI exempted all its houses from payments of every kind.

We have already seen John Fisher setting aside a part of his income in order to help poor scholars. Before that, he had been confessor to Lady Margaret Beaufort, the mother of Henry VII, whose wise and munificent gifts earned for her the title : " the greatest benefactress Cambridge has ever known." Fisher was the inspiration of these benefactions. It was he who induced Erasmus to lecture there in Greek at a time when the university was changing from an ancient to a modern seat of learning.

When Simon of Sudbury became Archbishop of Canterbury, he did not forget his native town, but founded and endowed a college on the site occupied by the house in which he had been born.

The majority of the students who frequented the medieval universities were poor, so poor that, between lessons, they had to drudge in order to keep body and soul together. Their plight it was that brought into being an extensive system of patronage both individual and collective. Benefactors endowed loan-chests and founded exhibitions ; until eventually the " colleges " were established. These " colleges " were in reality hostels or subsidized homes in which needy students were provided with bed and board. Grossteste was the son of poor parents and, consequently, owed everything to patronage. He never forgot the fact and, when he was in a position to do so, he became a patron in his turn. He assisted Roger Bacon and later encouraged him to become a Franciscan friar. Any lad who showed more than uncommon ability could count on finding some person or corporate body eager to advance his education. Richard Rolle of Hampshire, the solitary mystic, was one such. He was so bright a schoolboy that the Archdeacon of Durham undertook to send him to Oxford and to support him while there.

Indeed, at the time of the Dissolution, one of the grievances exploited by the Pilgrimage of Grace was the fact that there would now be no place left in which ordinary people's children could be educated. Later still, Bishop Latimer, in his *Sermon on the Ploughers*, roundly denounced the city of London men for neglecting to do what their forefathers did as a matter of duty. " In times past, the rich maintained the poor scholar, but now that the

knowledge of God's word is brought to light, almost no man is
willing to help."

In season and out did St. Edmund Rich labour to curb the
spirit of violence which was the curse of medieval Europe. In
that factious age he stood forth as a peace-maker and a preacher
of peace, pleading for concord between Christians, since He who
was the object of their faith had spent so much of Himself out of
love for them. It was a factious age enough. The murderer
whom Dante found in the seventh circle of Hell was Guy, son of
Simon de Montfort, Earl of Leicester. He was expiating the
murder of Henry of Cornwall. It was an act of private revenge,
and was done in Viterbo, and done during the actual celebration
of Mass. The heart of the victim was later brought home and
set in a gold cup upon a pillar at the end of London Bridge, to
keep the English in mind of the outrage. That such things should
be favoured by baptized Christians filled the soul of the archbishop
with indignation. And so, in his *Constitutions* he appeals particularly to the clergy.

" My sons ! an urgent necessity lies on us of cultivating and
fostering a peaceable disposition. Our God is the author and lover
of peace who came to perform a work of reconciliation. Therefore
do you strive your utmost to compose all quarrels and differences
that may arise among your flock."

Two monastic movements in particular are intimately associated with our English saints, the Cistercians and the Gilbertines.
The contributions which the first of these made towards the
development of civilization are notorious. Their libraries were
rich in books and manuscripts. Nor did they neglect the fine
arts ; they were foremost in the movement which propagated
Gothic architecture throughout our Continent ; they cultivated
painting and engraving. Rich they certainly became ; but their
wealth was, for the most part, used for the general good. Each of
their abbeys had a hostel for the poor and an infirmary for the sick

The acquisition of large properties by these communities may
have created a social problem ; but there can be no doubt that

this ownership was, in the first instance and for long, a social blessing. These monks were the first to cultivate waste ground on a big scale, to drain the marshes, make the roads, and restrain rivers and streams within bounds. In this way, they brought the greater part of Europe under cultivation. Then again, civilization could never have made such progress unless and until there was some sort of stability of tenure. In those days, attacks on property were as frequent as attacks on persons. The first thing to do to remedy this evil was to locate and fix the population by means of the agricultural life. The next thing was to teach people to respect property, not only by reasons drawn from morality but also by the actual sight of large establishments, belonging to corporate bodies, obliged to minister them equitably and with an eye to the common good. One result of slavery was that it produced a widespread contempt for manual labour. The Fathers of the Church employed all their eloquence in combating this prejudice, but it was the example of the monks, especially the Benedictines, that practically wiped it out. It is related of Becket himself that, as archbishop, he was in the habit of lending a hand whenever he chanced to be visiting a monastery during harvest time.

St. Wulstan, that prelate of large-hearted charity, is memorable on account of the successful efforts he made to withdraw his countrymen from the practice of trading in slaves. As everybody knows, the mission of Augustine which did so much to effect the conversion of the English, was the result of the appearance of a group of young Angles exposed for sale in the market-place of Rome. This circumstance made a deep impression upon the minds of our forefathers. At an early date, laws both civil and ecclesiastical were passed prohibiting the selling of Christians to Jews and pagans. Later, it was enacted that no persons who were innocent of crime should ever be sold out of the country. At all events, amongst us the trade never reached the dimensions of a national vice until the eighteenth century; a fact which, surely, must be put to the credit side of the medieval account.

5

Nevertheless, the record of the Middle Ages was not altogether unblemished, as we gather from Wulstan's *Life*. It is to his biographer, a certain sub-prior of Worcester called Hemming, that we are indebted for an account of the saint's preaching activities amongst the merchants of the west country. But for this passage, we might never have known that there was a time when the English made money by trafficking in their own flesh and blood. " At Bristol," says the chronicler, " you might have seen with sorrow long ranks of young persons of both sexes tied together with ropes, and daily exposed for sale. Some there were who even gave up their nearest relations, nay their own children in this way. But Wulstan made so great an impression on their minds that he induced them to abandon that wicked trade."

Wulstan's resounding eloquence did more. It induced William the Conqueror to draw up an enactment making the whole business illegal; and this is one of the many instances that might be adduced where the social legislation of the State was inspired by the reforming zeal of the Church.

THE GREAT TRAGEDY

THOSE of us who were brought up on Alban Butler will be sorry to hear that Becket's mother was not a Saracen lady after all. The medievalists, at close grips with the mysterious East, had a fancy for this sort of fiction; the thing is found amongst the early short stories of Italy, and in the romantic literature of later Spain. The idea of a Mohammedan falling in love with a Christian knight, following him across the world, and then being married to him, with baptism as a preliminary, had a glamorous appeal in those days. It was the medieval equivalent of a Hollywood film-star marrying an European nobleman—more or less, the difference being that in the former case the marriage lasted. Naturally, the ballads improved on the original story. In one of these, which bears the name of *Lord Beichan*, the Mohammedan damsel, who is called Susie Pye, follows her lover to Scotland and discovers him on the point of being married to another. However, the other is promptly dismissed and Susie Pye becomes Mrs. Becket.

But the martyr's mother, it seems, was a Norman like his father. This father, whom Butler very politely calls Mister Becket, was a city of London man. Well enough off, he never ought to amplify his means by money-making or commercial speculation. There was some slackness about the Saint's youth, but once when hunting he narrowly escaped drowning, and this caused him to pull himself together. Nor was there any occasion for further warnings of this kind. The living Becket had plenty of enemies, some of whom were of his own household; and the dead Becket has had plenty of critics; but no serious charges have ever been brought against his private life. His worth has been acclaimed by Protestants and Catholics alike. " With all his faults," says Professor Freeman, " he is fairly entitled to a place among the worthies of whom England is proud." Lord Campbell, in his *Lives of the Lord Chancellors*, describes him as

" one of the most distinguished men of any race that this island has yet produced " ; while Dean Hutton admits that " he was incomparably the most popular hero of the Middle Ages : and he was a hero because he was a saint."

As chancellor, he was worldly enough in appearance, such appearance being part and parcel of the office. Two casks of beer figured among the presents he brought to the French Court, but casks of beer were not considered naughty in those days. On becoming primate, away went the worldliness and the beer-casks and everything else of a like kind, to make room for a mode of living attuned to the traditions of the ascetical bishops of the Anglo-Saxon Church. From now on, we get the recognizable pieties—nocturnal prayer-risings, meal-time abstemiousness, frugality in the matter of clothes, and a painstaking service rendered to the poor. It will startle some to learn that he carried a Bible about with him and read it too, at odd moments, without any by-your-leave of the Holy See. To this time belongs the hymn ascribed to his pen containing the curious lines :—

> Gaude Virgo, Mater Christi,
> Quae per *aurem* concepisti,
> Gabriele nuntio !

Becket, however, did not originate this beautiful image or conceit. It was naturally suggested by the title *Logos*, and is found in the writings of the early Fathers. An ancient painted window represents a dove hovering over the Virgin mother, while a ray of light passes from its beak to her ear which was the way of entry of the Word. His last sermon at Canterbury was on the text, always an ironic or at least a poignant one in our squabbling world, " Peace on Earth to Men of Good Will."

This is the man who was murdered in his own cathedral at vesper-time on December the twenty-ninth, 1170. Hundreds of times over, in hundreds of books and parchments, the tragic details have been rehearsed, finding their way into the *Sagas* of the Northmen. Thanks to a host of scribes and chroniclers, the scene comes to life before our eyes.

The shades of evening had fallen, and in the obscurity of the vast church which was broken here and there by a lamp glimmering before a shrine, Becket might easily have hid himself in the dark and intricate crypts underground, or beneath the roof of the old church. Each of these courses was suggested by his attendants; but he rejected them both, and turned boldly to meet the intruders, followed or preceded by his cross-bearer, the faithful Gryme, the only one who did not flee. A voice shouted : " Where is the traitor ? " Becket answered not, but when Reginald Fitzurse said: " Where is the archbishop ? " he replied, " Here am I, an archbishop but no traitor, ready to suffer in my Saviour's name." Addressing Fitzurse again, he said, " I have done thee many pleasures; why comest thou with armed men into my church ? " They then told him that he must instantly absolve the bishops, to which he replied that he would never do so until they offered satisfaction. The faithful Gryme interposed his arm to save his master, and had it broken and nearly cut off. With the blood running down his face, Becket clasped his hands and exclaimed : " To God, to St. Mary, to the patrons of this church and to St. Denis I commend my soul and the Church's cause." When he was dead one of the conspirators placed his foot on his neck and cried : " Thus perishes a traitor."

How such a deed of blood came to be perpetrated is an old story and a familiar; but it can hardly be passed over in a book of this kind.

At first and for some years, Becket and Henry II were genuinely attached the one to the other, so much so that they were said to have but one heart and one mind. They romped like a pair of schoolboys, rode together at the head of the army, and hunted side by side. A psychologist might see something unhealthy in this friendship, unhealthy not in any moral sense, but in a psychological one. It may have been the sort that is apt to fall assunder through its own top-heaviness. Such things do happen. One extreme begets another; and it is just possible that the seeds of Becket's later all-round intransigence and Henry's later personal vindictiveness were sown during this period of their connection the one with the other.

At all events, in the beginning and for long, they saw eye to eye. Each had the welfare of the nation very much at heart, and probably the King's early administrative reforms were inspired by his chancellor. He organized Henry's expedition to Toulouse. He so backed up the imposition of the scutage or money-contribution exacted from ecclesiastics in place of military service, that he was accused by these same ecclesiastics of grinding the Church under his heel. To the very limit of what his conscience allowed he identified himself with his master's interests. Tennyson puts these words in the mouth of the primate :—

> I served our Theobald well when I was with him :
> I served King Henry well as chancellor :
> I am his no more, and I must serve the Church.

" I am his no more, and I must serve the Church "—this is about the short and the long of the painful story.

About some of the points for which Becket contended it may be difficult for us to work up any excitement at all. One of them was the right of the Church to try all clerics who broke the law of the land. A great number were able to claim the title of cleric at that time, and the ecclesiastical tribunal was very lenient—a murderer, for instance, might be condemned to confinement in a monastery. Still this leniency cut both ways. If a layman killed a priest, the Church tried the culprit and was as lenient as ever. Oddly enough, the primate's murderers owed their lives to this very principle. No punishment beyond excommunication and an enforced pilgrimage to the Holy Land seems to have befallen them, simply because they had to be tried by the spiritual power which could pronounce no higher sentence than that of excommunication.

Again, from our angle of vision, much that Henry appeared to be combating, at least at certain stages of the dispute, may look uncommonly like clericalism. But when we view the quarrel and all kindred ones as a whole, it becomes evident that a single big principle was at stake, the principle, namely, that England was amenable to the common and recognized laws of the Church Catholic or universal. The idea of a secular ruler assuming control of spirituals had entered nobody's head as yet. In spite of the justified and angry criticism of abuses, the Papacy was still accepted as a dogmatic fact. Some of those most severely critical of St. Thomas have nothing but praise for St. Anselm ; yet these two prelates were at one on the general principle—to use the latter's own words—" it lieth with His Holiness to decide questions regarding the welfare of the Church." Every word of Anselm's letter to William Rufus would have been endorsed by Becket. " In the things that are God's, I will tender obedience to the Vicar of St. Peter ; in things touching the earthly dignity of my lord the King, I will to the best of my ability give faithful counsel and advice." Attempts have been made to represent the martyr as a reactionary endeavouring to stifle the aspirations of the national Church. But this " national Church " is an unhistorical creation begotten of wishful thinking, as Professor Pollard allows.

What is just possible is that the then existing relationship between State and Church stood in need of some adjustment. Civil rulers began by endowing the Church with temporalities, and ended by claiming the right to appoint and to control those who were going to administer them. This created a deadlock, for on the one hand the Pope felt it necessary to protect the Church from lay interference, while the secular prince felt that such interference was necessary if he were to govern at all. This was the basis of the celebrated contest known as the Investiture Dispute. And it is significant that, a few years before Becket was born, Pope Pascal II made a worth while attempt to settle the whole question by desecularizing the Church. However, the opposition to his plan within the Church herself was too strong to permit so revolutionary a measure to be carried out.

For all that, the murder was a cowardly and brutal crime, and a sacrilegious one at that. The fact that the martyr was canonized two years after his death is evidence of the importance Christendom attached to the stand he had made. And the further fact that the King did public penance, and did it sincerely, is evidence that he accepted much of the responsibility.

All the same, Henry was not a monster. Peter of Blois, Archdeacon of London, has left behind a sort of memoir of him from which we learn that he suffered from in-growing toe-nail, also that he kept slim by fasting and horse-riding. Every day he heard Mass. The last years of his life were consoled by his friendship with St. Hugh, a Carthusian, whom he had himself promoted to the see of Lincoln. Hugh had a genuine and tender affection for the monarch, and he was not the man to cultivate out-and-out rascals. The list of Henry's religious foundations is considerable, and he showed practical interest in the crusade by organizing the Saladin Tithe. No reign is richer in legal history. It was under him that feudalism was shaken and the administrative system took root. He actively promoted Trial by Jury. Henry's death bed was embittered by the rebellion of his sons, but he received the Last Sacraments before the end came. The chronicler thought that God wished to punish him severely in this world in order to show him mercy in the next. Bossuet, in his beautiful panegyric of St. Thomas, thought that the King's repentance was a kind of miracle wrought through the intercession of his victim.

A tremendous revulsion of feeling followed Becket's death. His cause became the cause, not only of England but of Europe. Henry II certainly found his opponent even more formidable dead than he had been when alive. When the news spread the excitement was prodigious. His old foe, the Archbishop of York, ascended the pulpit to describe the tragedy as an infliction of the divine vengeance, saying that Thomas had perished in his guilt and pride like Pharaoh. Other ecclesiastics suggested that the body of the traitor ought to be cast into a ditch or hung on a gibbet. But it was soon found that the public voice was too loud to be drowned in this manner. One by one, the primate's former enemies came to their sober senses and realized the frightful pass to which their vendetta had brought them. Henry's biographer, Peter of Blois, makes a significant confession. In a letter written soon after, he says : " We fools counted his life folly and whatever he did was, at the time, interpreted and turned to envy and hatred." And, of course, regarding the chief points for which he had contended, Becket's vindication was complete.

It is not to be wondered at that this Martyr's shrine became one of the richest in England ; it was made so by the offerings of the common people, who had a shrewd notion that his sacrifice had been made on their behalf. Thierry, the French historian, who was a liberal of the old school, appraised Becket as the vindicator of Saxon rights and liberties against Norman oppression ; while our own J. A. Froude, who was by no means favourably disposed towards the Catholic religion, regarded him as the people's bulwark against monarchical and baronial outrage. The circumstances of his death, combined with the extraordinary cult of which he became and continued to be the object, make him quite unique among English saints.

But he is unique besides by reason of the multitude of his biographers. Gervase of Canterbury and Roger of Hovenden were contemporaries, as well as Fitzstephen to whom, incidentally, we are indebted for a very realistic picture of twelfth-century London. A work edited for the *Rolls Series* under the title *Materials for the History of Thomas Becket* runs to seven volumes, while the *Norse Saga*, edited in the same series, runs to two. A modern book, dealing with his death and miracles alone, also runs to two volumes ; and we have separate works dealing with his Life before Consecration, his Relics, his Bones, and the Pilgrimages made to his Shrine. There is, then, nothing sketchy about the portrait of the martyr which has been bequeathed to us ; all that can possibly be known about a human being is known about St. Thomas, even down to the details of his personal appearance. " To look upon he was slim of growth and pale of hue, with dark hair, a long nose and a slightly-featured face. Blithe of countenance, too, was he, winning and lovable in conversation, frank of speech but, withal, slightly stuttering in his talk. He was, besides, of so keen a discernment and understanding that he could make difficult questions plain."

PROBABLE CANDIDATES

If there are those before 1066 whose inclusion in the calendar is somewhat puzzling to account for, there are those after 1066 whose exclusion is even more puzzling still. In the case of these latter, we have no reason to suppose that their chance has gone for good and all. The Church has a long memory and a faithful one ; and it has happened, again and again, that those dead and buried for centuries have at last been accorded the highest honours. Joan of Arc had to wait for nearly five hundred years. St. Osmund of Old Sarum came over with the Conqueror, yet his turn came only in 1457. Albert the Great died in 1280 ; he was beatified in 1622 and canonized in our times.

The case of Robert Grosseteste, Bishop of Lincoln, is sometimes brought forward as a clear instance of papal spitefulness getting the better of papal impartiality. He appears to have been well entitled to a place among our saints, but he was not *persona grata* at Rome because he had set his face steadfastly against what he conceived to be the abuses of the Roman Curia. Nor did he stand alone in this. We learn from a joint protest sent to the Holy See by the King, barons and churchmen, that the bulk of the Italians enjoying English benefices did not reside in the country, and took no trouble to appoint substitutes. At this period, it is true, the Holy See was battling with the emperor, and needed money. Grosseteste was well aware of this, and what he objected to chiefly was the method employed for raising it.

And he had other grievances. He complained that those whom he found it necessary to censure had only to weight their appeal to Rome with a heavy bribe in order to succeed. Then, in the last years of his life, Innocent IV nominated one of his nephews to a vacant canonry in Lincoln, and threatened with excommunication any who dared to oppose him. Grosseteste did oppose him. He was not excommunicated all the same. He did incur papal suspension, but that was on another occasion. Indeed, the justice of his remonstrance was recognized in the end, and Innocent IV saw to it that the English bishops were able to be masters in their own house. At home, the good bishop was roundly accused of being a baiter of monks. He did make enemies amongst these, and he was actually excommunicated by the Benedictines of Canterbury; but there is no evidence that this hostility was provoked by unjust or vindictive measures. In his first visitation, he deposed seven abbots and five priors. In every case but one the grounds of complaint were not moral but disciplinary. What he found was that more than two-thirds of the parish churches of his diocese were in the hands of the monasteries; and these, in many instances, made little or no proper provision for the care of souls. That he was no wanton persecutor of religious is surely proved by his life-long love of and interest in the Franciscans who arrived at Oxford in his time.

Grosseteste's laugh was, by all accounts, a thing to be remembered; and he is credited with the saying that laughter is one of the requisites of sound health. St. Thomas More would have found in him a kindred spirit. They were devoted to the same causes; and, while both were unswerving in their loyalty to faith and fatherland, they were keenly aware of the abuses disfiguring Church as well as State. At death, the mind of each was clouded with anxiety as to the future of their country. Each, too, was something of a socialist, for while the one was the author of *Utopia* the other was the life-long friend of Simon de Montfort, a fact which popular contemporary ballads took care to stress. Again, each held a high position in the realm and, for much the same reasons, found his relations with the civil powers unusually strained.

When Robert Grosseteste died everybody over here acclaimed his sanctity and general greatness, everybody with the possible exception of the Canterbury monks. Miracles were wrought at his tomb, which became a place of pilgrimage. His canonization was demanded by Edward I and by Oxford University as a whole, but it was refused. Still it would be rash to assume that the motive of this refusal was just pique. St. Hilary of Arles carried on a spirited conflict with Pope Leo the Great, but the former was as good as canonized by the latter shortly after his death. Perhaps if the English had themselves beatified Grosseteste, the matter might have been allowed to remain at that. This very thing did happen in the same century and under the very eyes of the Papacy, when Jacopone, the Franciscan poet, who had been excommunicated by the pope, was publicly beatified at Todi, a town in the papal province. And, indeed, Edmund Rich, the Archbishop of Canterbury, strove long and hard to keep these foreign influences out of the Church of England, and he was canonized four years after his death.

Although no steps of any kind appear to have been taken in favour of Walter Hilton, miracles were reported at the tomb of his fellow mystic, Richard Rolle. A Mass and an Office were composed in his honour and other preparations made, but there the matter was allowed to rest. Others there were, too, who might have found a place in the calendar ; Richard the leper, for example, who was born at Wallingford, became Abbot of St. Albans, was highly skilled in the liberal sciences and mechanical arts, and was renowned for his sanctity.

And so we come to Henry VI. There is a portrait of him in the National Gallery. Looking at it, one feels that all that is wanting to complete it is a halo or nimbus. As soon as the news of his murder leaked out, he was venerated as a martyr by the Catholics of the north. And, martyr or no martyr, by the time the first of the Tudors ascended the throne, it was felt generally that if Edward the Confessor was to have a successor at all, Henry VI it must be. They were two for a pair in many ways. Each detested war, each kept clear of avarice—a species of heroism in a king—and each refused to burden the people with taxation. Judged by customary standards, neither of them was a strong ruler. Both seemed more suited to the cloister than the court. Henry would not allow swords to be worn in church, nor business of any kind to be transacted in the sacred edifice. His whole career of fifty years is marked by a pathetic naïvety, a certain innocent immaturity. What his deficiencies of intellect were it is not possible to say with any degree of certainty. It is conjectured that he may have inherited some portion of the malady that afflicted his maternal grandfather, but this manifested itself in a fear of responsibility and an infirmity of purpose rather than in unsoundness of mind. The energy of his race appears to have been extinguished in him. His life was a prolonged pupilage or submission to wills stronger than his own. He was born to a most unhappy position, and was subjected to a discipline that took no account of the gentleness and sensitiveness of his temperament.

Succeeding to the throne when he was nine months old, a little later he issued a letter patent authorizing Dame Alice Butler to attend his person " with due licence to chastise us reasonably from time to time." This sort of corporal punishment was the recognized instrument of good education in the fifteenth century. The scourge was strongly recommended, and there is extant a letter from one mother commanding her son's tutor to " belash him until he shall amend, for I had rather he were fairly buried in his grave than be lost for default." The people of London saw their little king, then two years old, carried shrieking and struggling and refusing to be held. Two years after, they saw him placed before the high altar in St. Paul's and then paraded through the city on a horse. Next he was conveyed to the House of Lords and seated on a throne on his mother's knees ; " a strange sight," says the chronicler, "and one never before seen in England."

Before he was five, we find Henry writing to the Pope petitioning for the canonization of Osmund of Salisbury. He was crowned when he was nine. At twenty-four he married Margaret of Anjou, after spending three days at the shrine of Guthlac of Croyland.

After the battle of Tawton, he fled to Scotland. Taken at last, he was thrown into the Tower ; and, about the hour of midnight on Tuesday, May the twenty-first, 1471, he was secretly assassinated by Richard Duke of Gloucester. His body was exposed in St. Paul's, where it bled in the sight of the beholders. It bled again at Blackfriars and all the way to Chertsey. While the details of his private life were still fresh, his chaplain, John Blackman, threw them into a memoir which may have been compiled for canonization purposes. Besides this, we have the *Book of the King's Miracles*, a copy of which—Cranmer's copy, it seems—is in the British Museum. Yet the cause of the founder of Eton and King's College, Cambridge, missed fire, probably owing to the distraction and embarrassments which at this time began to accumulate around the Holy See. But it had the backing of Henry VII and of all the best elements in the nation.

In easier times, something might have been done with the cause of Margaret Beaufort, the mother of Henry VII. During her life she was regarded as the pride of English matrons, " the holiest, most learned and noblest lady in the land." The victory of Bosworth Field, that ended the Wars of the Roses, was largely ascribed to her patriotic plotting. She was a small person in nothing except stature, and a tribute to her worth is to be found in the devoted attachment of a man like St. John Fisher. He became her chaplain and confessor in 1502, an honour to which he was to pay a generous tribute later on. " Though she chose me as her director, yet I gladly confess that I learnt more from her great virtue than ever I could teach to her." Fisher it was who pronounced the funeral oration of one who, to use his own words, " could never be praised enough."

Richard Challoner began his priestly work in London in 1730 when he was thirty-nine years of age. Though the penal laws were no longer enforced with extreme severity, he was obliged to celebrate Mass in obscure ale-houses, cockpits and wherever small gatherings could assemble without exciting remark. His zeal for souls carried him into the slums, the prisons, and the sponging-houses. As Vicar Apostolic of the London district, which at that time included ten counties besides the Channel Islands, he travelled almost incessantly, devoting himself to literary work in the interval. He had a narrow escape at the time of the Gordon Riots and, in fact, never recovered from the shock of that disaster. His private life was marked by extraordinary mortification and prayerfulness. He was credited with the gift of prophecy. His body lay in the churchyard at Milton, Berkshire, until 1946, when it was transferred to the crypt of Westminster Cathedral.

Whatever may be the chances of these and others like them, there are good grounds for expecting that the cause of the English Martyrs will be settled at no very distant date. The names of three hundred and sixty of these were forwarded to Rome in 1874. Twelve years later, by a decree of the Holy See, three hundred and sixteen of them were " approved " and " introduced," the other forty-four being postponed for further evidence of actual martyrdom. Soon after, another important decision was made. Sixty-three of the " approved " were recognized as having been equivalently beatified by the act of Pope Gregory XIII who, in 1583, had allowed the representation of their martyrdom to be painted on the walls of the English College in Rome. These sixty-three are, therefore, now honoured under the title of Blessed. Of the remaining number, one hundred and thirty-six were " raised to the altar " in 1929, and two of them, St. John Fisher and St. Thomas More, were solemnly canonized in St. Peter's in 1935. The present position, therefore, amounts to this that, apart from the forty-four who have been postponed, there are one hundred and thirty-six waiting to be canonized, and one hundred and sixteen waiting to be beatified.

THEIR CULTURE

It will be recalled that St. Wulstan's resignation was demanded on the score that he had not been well educated. And it will be recalled that the good man's defence was so ready and so ably-worded that his highbrow critics had nothing to say. Wulstan, in fact, is a standing refutation of the theory that the Church of God can be served, and well served, only by those whose intellectual attainments are outstanding.

Nevertheless, it must be conceded that, at this time, the standard of clerical education was not high. The period is the tail-end of the Iron Age which succeeded the dissolution of the Carlovingian Empire, when warfare, rapine and violence undermined society and all cultural institutions. The tenth century has been called the saddest in Christian annals, a century during which Christ was as if asleep in the vessel of the Church. And education suffered as much as anything else.

But this darkest hour proved to be the one before the dawn. The three hundred years succeeding the Conquest were marked by a devouring desire to learn, so much so that some authorities do not hesitate to describe them as the Golden Age of Intellectual Cultivation. In medieval England, the number of schools in proportion to the population was very great indeed, and so was the number of pupils attending. This closely-knit and country-wide system it was that enabled so many of our saints to reach the highest eminence in Church and State, quite irrespective of their social standing. Of course, the sons of well-to-do parents —for instance, St. Aelred, Gilbert of Sempringham, St. Thomas Becket, St. Simon Stock, St. Thomas of Hereford, and so on—had to pay something, but it was not a great deal. It is on record how the daughter of a certain Lady Beaumont received a convent education at the rate of £2 13s. 4d. *per annum*, while one Thomas Hunter paid 17s. 4d. a year for each of his children.

Robert Grosseteste or Big Head was a poor man's son, yet he became perhaps the most all-round product of the whole Anglo-Norman period; a teacher, a reformer, a scientist and a humanist —so much so that he has been called the Father of the Christian Renaissance. He knew Greek and made translations from it and, rare thing at that time, he had some acquaintance with Hebrew. He wrote a treatise on estate-management; he had unusual tastes; he has left behind an interesting collection of sermon notes. His works include studies in meteorology, light, colour and optics. He found fault with the Julian calendar, and thus paved the way for Pope Gregory's reform. He is credited with one of the earliest ideas for a microscope. He played a great part in the framing of the regulations and statutes which determined the character of Oxford University. In honour of the Virgin Mother and her Son, he wrote a poetic allegory of nearly two thousand lines in romance, that is to say, in the vulgar or early French tongue. Wyclif ranked him above Aristotle; John Gower, Chaucer's friend, the poet whose tomb is in the Protestant Cathedral of Southwark, called him " a grete clerc "; Roger Bacon hailed him as the only scientist of his age. " At this time," he wrote, " no one really knew the sciences except the Lord Robert, Bishop of Lincoln, by reason of his years and experience, as well as studiousness. Mathematics and perspective he knew, and there was nothing that he was unable to know. At the same time, he was sufficiently acquainted with languages to be able to understand the wise men of antiquity."

We may perhaps regret that Grosseteste was never canonized; no better compliment could have been paid to that long line of English medieval prelates who were, almost without exception, enthusiastic cultivators and patrons of learning.

St. Stephen Harding commenced his studies at the free school at Sherborne, where a teaching body has existed for over twelve hundred years, although the present establishment dates from the reign of Edward VI. From this humble beginning, he rose to become the co-founder of a religious order which, within the space

6

of half a century, counted no fewer than three hundred and fifty
abbeys, besides lesser houses dependent on the abbeys. At the
same time, it must be remembered that Stephen was not educated
for the cloister ; he entered and left Sherborne without any idea
of being a monk. St. Aelred, too, who became one of the most
eminent of medieval preachers, was what is called " a late vocation "
yet already, as a layman, he was in possession of a sound education
which included a knowledge of the classics. St. Gilbert of
Sempringham, being ill-favoured and deformed, was destined for
a military career—no great compliment to soldiers. His father,
who was a wealthy Norman settler, nevertheless spent a good
deal of money on the boy's education, even sending him as far
as Paris.

St. Edmund Rich became primate, and one of the brightest
ornaments of the kingdom, and yet his father was a tradesman
and, according to some, in a very small way at that. The boy
was sent, first to the abbey school at Abingdon, and then to the
university, a teaching establishment which, as such, was taking
definite shape at this very time. Paris was the forerunner, and
may be said to have been properly founded when the already
existing schools and professors united to form one teaching body.
This was in the last quarter of the twelfth century. The same
evolution took place at Oxford, where the schools of Saxon times
developed into a corporate institution. True, a certain enthusiastic chronicler assigned its origin to the time when Samuel was
judge in Judea, but it is now agreed that he was a little out in his
dates. Out also was the other ingenious gentleman who proved,
up to the hilt, that the founders of it were certain philosophers
who accompanied the Trojans in their conquest of our Island.
Such pedigrees were all the fashion in bygone days before the
human imagination had exhausted itself, the record being held
by an Irish family-tree in which there occurs a break with a foot-
note added : " About this time occurred the Deluge."

Of how St. Edmund fared at Paris we can form a fairly good
idea, because the life lived by the 'varsity student of those first

days has been reconstructed for us by a modern writer. His account runs more or less as follows. At five or six o'clock each morning the great cathedral bell would ring out the summons to work. From the neighbouring houses of the canons, from the cottages of the townsfolk, from the taverns and hospices and boarding houses, the stream of the industrious would pour into the enclosure beside the cathedral. The master's beadle, who levied a precarious tax on the mob, would strew the floor of the lecture hall with hay or straw, according to the season, bring the master's text-book, with the notes of the lecture between lines or on the margin, to the solitary desk, and then retire to secure silence in the adjoining street. Sitting on their haunches in the hay, the right knee raised to serve as a desk for the waxed tablets, the scholars would take notes during the long hours of the lecture (about six or seven), then hurry home—if they were enthusiasts—to commit the notes to parchment while the light lasted. The lecture over, the stream would flow back across the Little Bridge, filling the taverns and hospices, and pouring out over the great playing meadow that stretched from the island to the present Champ de Mars. All the games of Europe were exhibited on that international play-ground : running, jumping, wrestling, hurling, fishing and swimming in the Seine, tossing and thumping the inflated ball—a game on which some minor poet of the day has left us an enthusiastic lyric.

That the scholastic atmosphere was charged with a certain liveliness we gather from a report drawn up by Cardinal de Vitry in the actual lifetime of St. Edmund. According to this, " almost all the students at Paris, foreigners and natives, did absolutely nothing except learn or hear something new. Some studied merely to acquire knowledge, which is curiosity ; others to acquire fame, which is vanity ; still others for the sake of gain, which is cupidity and the vice of simony. Very few studied for their own edification or that of others. They wrangled and disputed, not merely about the various sections and subjects of discussion, but the differences between the countries also caused dissensions,

hatreds and virulent animosities among them, and they impudently
uttered all kinds of affronts and insults against one another. They
affirmed that the English were drunkards and had tails ; that the
sons of France were proud, effeminate and carefully adorned like
women. They said that the Germans were furious and obscene
at their feasts ; the Normans, vain and boastful ; the Poitevins,
traitors and always adventurers. The Burgundians they considered vulgar and stupid. The Bretons were reported to be
fickle and changeable, and were often reproached for the death
of Arthur. The Lombards were called avaricious, wicked and
cowardly ; the Romans, seditious, turbulent and slanderous ; the
Sicilians, tyrannical, brigands and ravishers ; the Flemings, fickle,
prodigal, gluttonous, yielding as butter and slothful. After such
insults as these in words they often came to blows."

Edmund was very much in earnest, we may be sure, and knew
how to take care of himself. Later he taught successfully in both
universities.

St. Richard of Chichester's case is even more remarkable
because, although his parents were gentle-folk, he had to work his
passage without financial assistance of any kind. Born at the
manor of Wyche or Wick, he is known as Richard de Wyche.
This Wyche is now Droitwich, the Droit, i.e. Right, being pre-
fixed to the old name by sanction of Edward III, who authorized
the people to manufacture salt there. This happened some fifty
years after the saint's death. In Chester and the neighbouring
districts, wich is the ending of most salt-producing towns, but
there appears to be no authority for believing that wich or wick
had anything to do with salt. Before the Conquest, Droitwich
was known as Saltwich.

Richard's father and mother died when their children were
quite small, leaving the family estates in charge of an incompetent
agent. But mere lad though he was, and the younger son, the
saint retrieved the family fortunes. His elder brother then
wished to resign the inheritance to him with a wealthy bride
thrown in as an extra, but Richard said No, and walked off to

Oxford with only a few coppers in his pocket. He shared a room with another student and, since they could only afford a single gown between them, one stayed in bed while the other attended the lectures, and *vice versa*. They were often short of food, and the only heating apparatus they possessed was their own energy, but they were as happy as sand boys for all that. From Oxford to Paris he went, and then back to Oxford for his M.A. degree, and so to Bologna, the chief law school of those days, where budding barristers were taught the Dictamen or Rules for drawing up briefs. Here it was that Gratian taught, the founder of the science of Canon Law. The motto of the city was a proud one : *Bononia Docet—Bologna Does Teach*. Later, the holder of a Bologna diploma was entitled to teach everywhere and anything without further examination or licence. When Richard arrived, there were ten thousand students drawn from every part of Europe, and these had the right to elect the Rector. Richard spent seven years in Bologna. He might have stayed longer, only one of his tutors took such a fancy to him that he wanted to make him his heir and, incidentally, his son-in-law. For the second time in a dozen years he found himself declining a legacy and a lady. But he was taking no risks and, consequently, returned to Oxford.

Almost at once, he was made chancellor of the university and, soon after, chancellor to the Archbishop of Canterbury, Edmund Rich, already being harassed to death by Henry III. He accompanied that prelate on his voluntary exile into France and nursed him until his death. Of these two a contemporary said : " Each leaned upon the other ; saint upon saint ; master upon disciple and disciple upon master." We next hear of Richard at Orleans in a convent of Dominicans where he was ordained priest and next, again, at Dover, where he was in charge of a parish.

Eventually he was made Bishop of Chichester, and in that capacity suffered more than he had done as a student in Paris. He died suddenly at Dover. His last words were " Into Thy hands, O Lord, I commend my spirit," followed by one verse of a hymn in honour of Christ's Blessed Mother. He was only fifty-five, and was canonized by Urban IV, a Pope who was the son of a shoemaker.

The priests among the English Martyrs were, for the most part, trained in foreign seminaries or religious houses, yet of that noble band no fewer than sixty-three were Oxford University men. There is one great poet amongst them, Robert Southwell the Jesuit, who was hanged at Tyburn in 1595. Most of his poems were written in prison, and of one of them, *The Burning Babe*, Ben Jonson declared that he would have been well content to destroy any of his own for the sake of this one. Southwell, in fact, was the only purely religious poet of his age. Edmund Campion's father was a London bookseller—not a very remunerative occupation in those days. The boy was educated at the expense of one of the City companies, first at a grammar school and then at Christ-Church Hospital. Sir Thomas Whyte, the lord mayor, who built and endowed St. John's College, Oxford, accepted Campion as one of his first pupils. As a mere stripling, he had been chosen to deliver the Latin oration when Mary Tudor entered London. Other orations followed later on at Oxford ; one for the reburial of Amy Robsart, the tragic heroine of Scott's *Kenilworth*, and another for the funeral of the founder of the college to which Campion belonged. " Every tradition, every remnant of his written words, and not least his unstudied golden letters, show that he was nothing less than a man of genius, truly one of the great Elizabethans." When he left the country in order to study for the priesthood, Cecil lamented the exportation of " one of the diamonds of the kingdom."

More's literary accomplishments are well known. His fame as a writer rests on a book generally called *Utopia* (*Nowhere*), but the lengthy title which the author himself gave to the work actually does not include that famous name. *Utopia* was written in Latin, but More is rightly regarded as one of the makers of English prose. He was a great deal besides. His educational career started at St. Anthony's free school in Threadneedle Street, continued in

the household of Cardinal Morton at Lambeth Palace, and
finished at Canterbury College (now Christ Church) Oxford,
where he was so short of money that he had to write home as
often as his shoes needed mending.

St. John Fisher, being a native of Beverley, no doubt began
his education at the school attached to the Minster, an establishment dating from the reign of Athelstan, and one that was em-
powered to confer degrees in grammar. When he was about
fourteen, he went to Cambridge and became a member of Michael
House, the second oldest college in the university, and one of the
ancestors of Trinity. Student life here was no different from
that at Paris. There was plenty of poverty, plenty of hard work,
and plenty of fighting. In due course, Fisher took his B.A., his
M.A., his D.D. Eventually he was elected Senior Proctor, Vice-
Chancellor and Chancellor. As Bishop of Rochester, his greatest
natural happiness was found in his library, which was said to
contain the finest private collection of books in England. These
he intended for his poor college of St. John's, Cambridge, and
he did, in fact, make them over by a deed of gift; but, as soon as
he had been attainted and cast into prison, the royal commissioners looted his scanty belongings and played havoc with his
library. Providentially enough, this man—so devoted to books—
found in one book his final sustenance and consolation. On his
way to the scaffold, he opened his New Testament in the hope
that he might find that in it needful for his present comfort. At
once his eye fell upon the Master's prayer for His disciples:
"This is eternal life, that they may know Thee, the only true
God, and Jesus Christ Whom Thou hast sent. I have glorified
Thee on earth: I have finished the work that Thou gavest me
to do." Closing the book, he said: "Here is learning enough for
me to my life's end."

RENUNCIATIONS

Voluntary privations in plenty we find amongst them, even in the matter of food and drink, a species of self-denial that does not come easily to those among the English in whom the Anglo-Saxon strain predominates. The early Norman chroniclers comment on the gross eating habits of the natives. That things were slow in mending, we gather from Gerald de Barry, otherwise Giraldus Cambrensis, who describes a feast-day banquet at the Benedictine monastery in Canterbury consisting of sixteen courses. This was probably round about the year 1200.

St. Thomas of Hereford was a life-long martyr to colic and dyspepsia. Indeed, stomach troubles seem to have been the portion of the saints of this period, and we gather that what was to blame was the chronic incompetence of our English cooks. In one of his letters, Peter of Blois speaks feelingly of what even church dignitaries had to endure in this respect. " They have bread put before them which is not kneaded, not leavened, made of the dregs of beer, full of bran and unbaked—bread like lead. The beer itself is horrid to taste and filthy to look at. The wine is so full of lees, that you have to drink it with closed eyes and clenched teeth. Many more deaths would ensue from this murderous fare were it not that the famishing greediness of the stomach sucks it in like a whirlpool."

St. Simon Stock drank water only, while for food he ate herbs, roots and wild apples mostly. When St. Stephen Harding began his life at Citeaux, he and his lived on berries and pulse. This pulse, for which ascetics everywhere have had so strong a partiality, is defined by the learned as " the esculent seeds of leguminous plants." When Stephen later drew up his Rule, he made it as strict as it could be made, particularly in the matters of detachment and poverty. The curiosity of sight-seers was discouraged, precious ornaments were banished from the church, common cloth was prescribed for making the vestments, and it was forbidden to use chalices of gold.

"As to her eating," writes the biographer of St. Margaret, "it was so sparing that it barely sufficed to maintain life. She tasted rather than ate." The abstemiousness of St. Aelred was such that he is described as being more like a ghost than a man.

St. Wulstan renounced flesh meat and all because once, when saying Mass, he was distracted by the odour of a steak cooking in the nearby kitchen. Roots and pulse, too, were good enough for Gilbert of Sempringham. At meals, he had a dish placed on the table which he called "the platter of the Lord Jesus," and into it went a portion for the poor. Incidentally, this custom was enjoined upon monks and nuns from the earliest times. In one comparatively modern religious order, the members are supposed to leave something or other on the plate "for the Divine Infant," who in His turn passes it on to the beggars who congregate at the monastery door.

By our standards, Gilbert's subjects had a hard time of it. Two meals daily were allowed, but only one in winter because the days are shorter in winter. No flesh meat was eaten except by the sick, a restriction in line with the practice of some orders even at the present day; but there was beer for everybody. In imitation of the Blessed Virgin, the Office was chanted in a monotone, the figured variety of music being associated with Herodias and the perversion of weak minds. The organ was strictly prohibited. While yet a layman, Gilbert was presented to two livings in his father's gift, which meant that the actual work had to be done by curates while the cream of the revenue went to the presentee. However, that was the custom of the day, seemingly, and disturbed the conscience of very few. All the same, it disturbed Gilbert's conscience, for he used the proceeds of one benefice only and reserved the other for the poor. Soon after, he was ordained more or less against his will; but when he was offered the archdeaconry of Lincoln, he refused; and not politely either, for he roundly declared that he knew no surer road to perdition ; hence, perhaps, the famous doubt regarding the salvation-chances of archdeacons in general. When Grossteste was beginning his ecclesiastical career, dignities and preferments were showered upon him until, in the end, he was in possession of no fewer than four archdeaconries, besides several livings and one prebend. But a providential illness opened his eyes wide enough to be able to detect an evil which few eyes were able to see at that time. He resigned everything except the prebend.

Edmund Rich took the degree of Master of Arts and excelled in mathematics, the science of quantity and arrangement which draws necessary conclusions. Mathematics seems to resemble Catholicism in this that if you do not want it to grip you like a pair of pincers, you must leave it severely alone. It is either loved passionately or passionately hated. At all events, Edmund renounced it in the end, just as Pascal did, and he invented the arithmetical machine and demonstrated the weight of air, besides writing a treatise on sound when he was twelve, and one on conic sections when he was sixteen. Both renounced it and for the same reason. Both had, or thought they had, a vision in the night and that settled it. It was Edmund's deceased mother who appeared to him and asked him what profit he imagined there could be in knowing that a point has position and no magnitude, et cetera ? What profit, indeed ? Some of us asked that very question when we were young and foolish. With the dawning of the morning, the dutiful son drew a duster over the blackboard and gave himself up to theology. The moral might seem to be that you cannot serve God and Euclid which, as the latter would say, is absurd. Indeed, it happened once that one of Euclid's own pupils asked this same question : " What advantage shall I get by studying these things ? " and, by way of answer, the mathematician called his slave and bade him give the pupil twopence, " since he must needs make a profit out of what he learns." However, looked at in the proper light, if the heroism of renunciation derives from the value of the thing renounced, Edmund's was an heroic holocaust. Perhaps it was intended to harden him and prepare the way for the bigger sacrifice he was called upon to make before the end, the renunciation of his archbishopric and of his native land.

Certainly, to conclude that spiritual people embark upon penitential experiments with nothing in view save the hurting of themselves is just simplicity and, like many simplifications, only leads us astray. Altogether, Edmund was a pattern of detach-ment. As primate, he continued to dress and behave in a homely way, conduct which gave offence to some of his fellow-bishops. He was accused of being a back-number, of trying to resurrect the out-moded fashions of the early Church, when the chalices of the altar were made of wood and the ministers of the same made of gold. At Canterbury, he exercised hospitality to the full and kept a plentiful table; but he himself was expert in the art of making a show of eating. On Fridays, he contented himself with a meal of bread and water—a week to week abstinence which many modern dieticians would cordially approve. As a student, he slept either on the floor or on a bare bench, and for thirty years never undressed himself for sleep or used a bed. The one he had in his room was just a blind, and he would disarrange it in order to conceal his austerity. At midnight he rose for matins and then usually remained up until morning. One knack he did acquire, namely, that of sleeping on his feet with his head leaning against the wall.

Gilbert of Sempringham never lay down for sleeping purposes. This is recorded of several others. It cannot exactly be classed as an unusual form of penance, if indeed it be a form of penance at all. The Poor Clare does not lie down in bed; she reclines in a kind of half-sitting posture, and seems to sleep just as soundly as any of us. And, of course, we must not think of any of these saintly personages undressing at night, as we do, and changing into night-gowns and pyjama-suits. They more or less retired to rest as they were. Sleeping clothes were very unusual in the Middle Ages, and many of the illuminations in the manuscripts show the sleeper quite undressed. As for religious folk, the Rule of St.

Benedict furnished the general type of monastic bedding for centuries. The habit and girdle had to be worn, but the sleeper was allowed a mat, a blanket, a rug and a pillow.

The self-denial which Thomas Becket imposed upon himself as soon as he became archbishop is well known. When he was chancellor, he moved about on the King's business attended by a splendid retinue, just as, before him, Alcuin had done when he was employed by Charlemagne. For this, each in turn was sharply criticized. We do not know how Becket justified himself, but Alcuin's excuse may serve for both. Writing to his friend, the Bishop of Lyons, he says : " So-and-So takes me to task for my riches, servants and vassals who amount to the number of thirty thousand. But he ought to reflect that possessions are vicious only when they engage the heart. It is one thing to own the world and another to be owned by it ; and some who have but little, passionately covet much." A sensible enough reply, it must be admitted.

But Becket changed into a new man as soon as he reached Canterbury. On went the hair shirt, over which he put a Benedictine habit, and over that a canon's robe of light stuff. He rose during the night to pray, and in the morning washed the feet of the poor, giving them bread and meat. At his own table everything was of the plainest, although he saw that his guests had the best. A certain monk once found him eating the wing of a pheasant, and was scandalized thereat ; which shows the impossibility of pleasing some people.

This scandal may have been a take-over from earlier times when flesh meat of any description was considered *de trop* for those who had high spiritual aspirations. But, before 1066, there were long periods of scarcity during which this form of nourishment was cheaper than bread. Wheat was so dear that whole monasteries were compelled to use barley flour or, in defiance of tradition, turn to flesh meat. Rude methods of butchering, too, were in vogue so that the joints were of poor quality ; at any rate, coarse and indelicate. During one-half of the year the meat was salted. After the Conquest, bread, butter and cheese—the latter often made with ewes' milk—seem to have formed the staple diet of the poor people, since these articles have preserved their Anglo-Saxon names, whereas the various kinds of flesh-meat have Norman names, beef, pork, mutton, venison, and so on. What flesh the peasant had was mostly pig's flesh, eked out with the white meat of domestic fowls. And, of course, there would be vegetables, although not a great variety of these. Piers Plowman informs us that he has " two loaves of beans and bran baked for his children, as well as parsley, leeks and many cabbages." What we call root crops were not grown at that time. There was no beet, no cauliflowers, no broccoli, no carrots and very few turnips.

The Church has never favoured the taking of life of any kind by ministers of religion ; and, in the case of England, there was the added difficulty that the chase was indulged in mostly on Sundays, at any rate for some time. St. Wulfric broke this rule, but that was before his conversion. At one period, Thomas Becket was so enamoured of hawking that he neglected his very prayers. This was after his studies, when he was taken into the service of a certain country nobleman ; like master, like man. Then his eyes were opened. One day his hawk swooped down on a duck and dived after it into the river. The saint went to the rescue, and was carried by the current right under the wheel of a mill. But the wheel stopped of its own accord and Thomas never hunted again.

When Edmund Rich went off to Paris to finish his studies, his mother gave him a hair shirt as a parting gift. Later, into every tuck-box which she sent, went some instrument of penance. That these same shirts had very little respect even for the skins of arch-bishops is evident from a specimen piece that is still preserved intact, although it was actually worn by St. Thomas Becket. It is, or was, at Erdington, near Birmingham. The cloth is brown in colour, woven like a net and diversified by great knots.

St. John Fisher, as bishop, was in duty bound to the virtue of hospitality, but he took good care to see that all the titbits on the table went to his guests. He observed the fast days so rigorously that his health gave way, and he was obliged to relax to the extent of a plate of thin gruel. For thirty years he lived in the tumble-down palace at Rochester. Here Erasmus visited him, and afterwards wrote warning him not to expect anything but illness in such a habitation " in which I could not exist for three hours without being sick." But the bishop stuck to his post and abated none of his austerities. He slept for four hours only, and on a bed of straw and mats. When his goods were forfeited to the Crown, the commissioners found very little for their pains beyond a hair shirt and several well-used scourges.

ON THE HEIGHTS

THE fourteenth century was a bubbling cauldron of strangely contrasted ingredients. The pangs of birth and the agonies of death, ruin and reconstruction, hopes and fears, light and darkness —all are blended in it. We are here in the midst of the Black Death, the Great Schism, the Hundred Years' War, and the Peasants' Revolt—portents calculated to unseat the optimism of the most inveterate Utopianist. But it was also the age of Geoffrey Chaucer and John Gower, of Dante and Petrarch. And it was the age of Tauler and Suso, of Ruysbroeck and Gerard Groote, of Thomas à Kempis, and St. Catherine of Siena. The stress and calamity of the time did not hinder the Muse from descending nor yet the Paraclete. To these latter names we must add those of our own mystics, Juliana of Norwich, Walter Hylton, Richard Rolle, and the author of *The Cloud of Unknowing*.

This Black Death was so-called because of the dark blotches which appeared on the skin of the victims, although at first the symptoms manifested themselves in the form of tumours as large as common apples. China was held to be the starting-point of the visitation, which travelled westwards to the accompaniment of various cosmic phenomena of a very novel character. All classes were affected. Precautionary measures seem to have been unavailing, for Florence suffered as badly as any city in spite of the creation of an energetic staff of sanitary inspectors. On this side, in the first year, it carried off Edward III's daughter and, later, no fewer than three Archbishops of Canterbury.

On August the 1st, 1348, the disease made its appearance in Dorsetshire, and travelled slowly westwards and northwards through Devon and Somerset to Bristol. This latter town was then more or less placed in quarantine. It reached London on the Feast of All Saints. By New Year's Day it had spread to Norwich. We are told that, although it visited Canterbury, it spared the monks of Christ-Church because their prior had, a century before, laid on pure water from the hills to the monastery. Every town had its plague-pit, London's being later occupied by the Charterhouse. The loss of population throughout Europe is given as twenty-five millions. In England, it is probable that about one-third of the people perished, although, as usual, panic grossly exaggerated the mortality. The chronicles speak of whole towns being wiped out, just as did our gossips during the air raids.

This avalanche of misfortune had serious repercussions in the moral and spiritual spheres. It is customary to assert that in times of grave calamity people turn to God. Some certainly, even many perhaps; but not all. Boccaccio's account of the Black Death as it affected Italy or, at least, the city of Florence, ranks as one of the finest descriptive passages that literature contains. And while he begins by a Christian confession of belief that the scourge came as a providential corrective, he describes in detail the effect it actually had on numbers who affirmed that the sovereign antidote was to drink deep, satisfy every appetite, and mock and ridicule everything. "And as they said, so they did. Night and day, now at one tavern now at another, onward they went inbibing without mode or measure, and living in a condition of brutish sensuality." In the case of England, we are assured that, if anything, it made the powerful more oppressive than ever, the rich more covetous, and the licentious more abandoned.

The plague, coupled with the decay and confusion that followed, undid the patient, laborious work of centuries. The demoralization extended to every department. The land went out of cultivation through dearth of workers; and the measures taken to retrieve the position were so unpopular, that they provoked the rising under Wat Tyler. The whole spirit of society was altered for the worse. The universities practically closed down. The depleted ranks of the clergy were hastily filled up with unsuitable and badly educated candidates, so that the

Church found herself stricken by weakness at the very time that hostile forces were everywhere being set in motion against her.

However, in accordance with some mysterious law of equilibrium, it was just then, when the Middle Ages were coming to an end in a welter of travail and agony, that God allowed the heavens to open and its innermost secrets to be revealed. The mystics, after all, are the pawns which He places on the chess-board of the world at His will. It is their part to abandon themselves body and soul to Him who directs them. And it is their vocation to effect a radical transformation of humanity by setting an example; at least, that is how their function is interpreted by a modern philosopher who will be quoted later on. They are the far shining initials that illuminate the ordinary text of Christian lore. They show forth in living pictures, as once did the Bibles of the unlearned, such phrases as " Seek ye first the kingdom," " One thing is necessary," " I am thy reward exceeding great." Their existence bears witness, with the wordless might of fact, that God is God, the Master and the Beloved of mankind. We all live on the shores of God's sea ; but they are the intrepid vikings who fare forth and surrender themselves to all its terrors and wonders.

It stands to reason that there were many before this time who reached very high degrees of prayerfulness. There is Edmund Rich for one. He is reported to have fallen more than once into a rapture, that is to say a condition of mental transport or exultation such as St. Paul experienced : " Whether in the body or out of the body, I know not ; God knoweth." Once when dinner had been announced and his chancellor went to the chapel to call him, he found him raised above the ground in ecstasy. We are informed that he directed many in the ways of contemplation, insisting always and above all that our prayer should be interiorized to the best of our ability. He was fond of quoting the verse of the Psalm : " Sing to the Lord wisely," against those who, after the fashion of Ben Gunn in *Treasure Island*, rattle along so fast that they cannot tell one word from another. " A hundred thousand persons," he would say, " are deceived in multiplying prayers. I would rather repeat five words with my heart, than five thousand which my soul does not relish with affection and understanding. What we repeat with the mouth, that we must feel inwardly." Edmund left behind a spiritual tract called *The Mirror of the Church* which contains many wise reflections concerning the great business of raising the mind and heart to God, and his name is set down in an eighteenth-century dictionary of mystical writers. One authority assures us that he was inured to contemplation from his youth.

There is St. Aelred, as well, who ranks among the mystics of the twelfth century, and was known as the English St. Bernard; and there is St. Walthen who, like St. Paul, was once caught up to the third heaven. All the same, the fourteenth century is unique in this that it is identified with a widespread revival of mystical systems. In fact, some maintain that the mysticism of this period is the finest and sanest that has ever been—the classic mysticism of the Christian Church.

Juliana was probably a Benedictine nun living as a recluse in a cell attached to the eastern portion of the church of St. Julian in Norwich. Nothing appears to be on record about her antecedents or early life, and her very name is obviously a nickname. That is to say, she comes before us simply and solely as the winged messenger of the highest truth, fully-fledged and anonymous. According to her own book, *Sixteen Revelations of Divine Love*, her visions or " shewings " began when she was just turned thirty; with the exception of a three months' interruption, they continued for twenty years. The starting point was a kind of trance into which she passed—while seemingly at the point of death—at a moment when she was contemplating an image of Christ crucified. In this trance, she saw the drama of our Saviour's sufferings being enacted before her, as did Blessed Angela of Foligno and Ann Catherine Emmerich. The *Sixteen Revelations* are the record of twenty years' meditation on this first vision " in which all the shewings that follow be grounded and joined." About fifteen years after this phenomenon, she came into possession of the master-key which unlocks everything, the secret and explanation of all things—Love.

> And in that depth
> Saw in one volume, clasp'd of Love, whate'er
> The universe unfolds; all properties
> Of substance and of accident, beheld,
> Compounded, yet one individual light
> The whole. And of such bond methinks I saw
> The universal form.

For it must be remembered that all the science of the Middle Ages is gathered up in Dante's great poem, its mystical science included.

In the light of this new revelation, the existence of evil and the possibility of sin no longer troubled Juliana, but " were made a bliss by love." That is to say, at this stage of her contemplation she—like her fellow mystics—was enabled to view all things in their finality and, therefore, they did not worry her as they do us who see them only incompletely. Those thus enlightened see the sequel as—let us say—a mother does who takes her child to the dentist. The child concentrates on the grim here-and-now actuality, and is troubled ; but the mother remains calm knowing that all's well that ends well. And, indeed, again and again Juliana tells us how clearly she saw that " all would yet be well."

This it is, no doubt, that explains the calmness that broods over the attitude of these spiritual people towards the tormenting drama of human life. Because their love for their Creator is intense, intense likewise is their love for their fellow creatures. But this love is very different indeed from the fiercely hysterical love of the extreme social reformer. His trouble is that he is usually a sort of atheist ; and those who are without God must become tragically, and even dangerously, important the one to the other. They are welded together not by a common supernatural destiny, but rather by a common doom and despair. Hence the contradictions of this despiritualized benevolence ; its blasphemies, its search for scapegoats, its refusal to recognize the place occupied by the Cross in the scheme of existence, its sullen anger against those who dare to go on believing in prayer and in providence. But "charity—Christian charity—is patient, is kind; it is not puffed up; it dealeth not perversely; it rejoiceth not in iniquity but rejoiceth with the truth."

Elsewhere in her book, Juliana lays special stress upon the "courtesy" and the "homeliness" of God's dealings with us, "for love makes His power and His wisdom full meek to us," and "in falling and in rising we are ever preciously kept in the one love." We are assured that "body and soul render mutual aid, each taking help of the other"; and again that "God is nearer to us than our own soul."

Richard Rolle, the hermit of Hampole, was a Yorkshireman born in the first year of the fourteenth century. He showed such promise as a lad that the Archdeacon of Durham undertook to defray the cost of his education at Oxford. However, at the age of nineteen, he left the university without completing his course, "for his soul's health," as he tells us—a left-handed compliment to that famous seat of learning. While determined to devote himself to a life of prayer and contemplation, he did not desire to enter a religious order. Instead, he buried himself in a wood near his home; but, eventually being fearful of his family's interference, he fled from the neighbourhood and entered a hermit's cell at Dalton. Here he attained to a high degree of contemplation, having passed through the well known preparatory stages; although, curiously enough, he describes the three phases as *Calor*, *Canor* and *Dulcor*. His ultimate condition of soul was such that, as he says, he did not think that "anything like it or anything so supernatural could be attained in this life." Richard wandered about a good deal before finally settling down at Hampole near Doncaster.

Walter Hylton of Nottinghamshire, who died towards the close of the same century, also passed through the mystical Dark Night which, he informs us, "is nought else but a turning away of the mind and soul from earthly things." This accomplished, our spiritual eyes are opened wide and are able to perceive God's very nature, as well as the operation of His will and design in human affairs. In short, Walter, like Juliana, found himself in possession of the master-key, so that—to use his own words—" he was able in one hour to apprehend more intimate truth and reality than could be elucidated by means of a great book." Nor does he anywhere manifest the slightest doubt or hesitation regarding the validity of this truth and this reality, a state of affairs very characteristic indeed of all such visionaries. Thus, referring to certain intellectual illuminations which he received in the cave at Manresa, St. Ignatius Loyola declared that, even had the Bible not existed, he would have felt ready to give his life for the faith that had come to him on the strength of the said revelations.

The familiar process by which these mystics emerge out of painful darkness into blissful light is well described by Bergson, the philosopher, who devoted the last years of his life to the study of mystical phenomena. "To analyze," he writes, "the final phase, characteristic of great mysticism, is impossible, for the mystics themselves have barely had a glimpse of the mechanism. Let us confine ourselves to suggesting that a machine of wonderfully tempered steel, built for some extraordinary feat, might be in a similar state if it became conscious of itself as it was being put together. Its parts being one by one subjected to the severest tests, some of them rejected and replaced by others, it would have a feeling of something lacking here and of pain all over. But this entirely superficial distress would only have to be intensified in order to pass into the hope and expectation of a marvellous instrument. The mystic soul yearns to become this instrument. It throws off anything in its substance that is not pure enough, not flexible and strong enough, to be turned to some use by God."

This work of preparation over a calm exultation of all its faculties makes the soul see things on a vast scale only. Above all, it sees things simply. Worry is no more. Problems vanish, darkness is dispelled. Everything is flooded with light. In the words of St. John of the Cross :

> I know the fountain ever springs and flows,
> Though night be dark and still.

Both Richard Rolle and Walter Hylton were practical mystics like Thomas à Kempis. That is to say, they passed on the fruit of their experience to those in the world, in order to show how people of affairs can unite themselves with God. Richard wrote many prose treatises, as well as a long poem entitled *The Prick of Conscience*. All are marked by intense personal feeling, sympathy and simplicity. He counsels moderation and discretion in everything, and says frankly that illness, fatigue and the strain of effort make contemplative prayer impossible. Sitting was his favourite posture in time of prayer. " Sitting I am most at rest and my heart most upward." Although he translated many parts of Scripture into English, only his version of the Psalms has been printed. The *Form of Living* is the best of his works, while the most popular is a mixed composition entitled *I sleep but my heart watcheth*.

In this century, the English tongue was coming into its own and the reading public was growing, so that these religious writings are characterized by a certain lucidity of expression and a sureness of touch. In style, Walter's works are almost modern. They are characterized throughout by clearness, high-thinking and, above all, a balanced judgement ; which confirms Bergson's opinion about the supreme good sense of mystics generally. One of his treatises is designed to show how seculars can make their life acceptable to God, and can even attain to a deep insight into the higher spiritual mysteries. *The Imitation of Christ* has been frequently assigned to his pen, the explanation being that that book reached England anonymously and, when translated, was naturally attributed to the spiritual writer whose name was a household word in this country.

To this same Walter has been attributed, on insufficient grounds, that remarkable book, *The Cloud of Unknowing*. The English of it is the Midland dialect used by Chaucer ; and the title is explained by the contents, whose whole point is that mystic contemplation pierces the cloud interposing between the human mind and perfect knowledge. In this work of spiritual genius, the depth of the thought is balanced by the simplicity of the style; as, for instance, where he says: "Take God as He is, pat and plain as a poultice, and lay Him on thy sick soul." His last message is replete with sterling comfort: "Not what thou art, nor what thou hast been seeth God with His eyes of Mercy, but rather what thou hast a mind to be."

A lesser known mystic is Margery Kempe, who appears upon the scene somewhat later. Her autobiography, in which she frankly discusses her difficulties and describes her pilgrimage to the Holy Land, was only brought before the public in 1940. She had read Hylton and Rolle, and knew Juliana personally. Of this work, the *Cambridge History of English Literature* says that it is the first autobiographical confession of its kind in our tongue, is a moving addition to the literature of religious experience, and shows English prose as clearly written in the fifteenth century as in the century of Foxe and Bunyan. Speaking of vocal prayer, Margery quotes for us the words of caution which she received from the lips of Christ Himself: "Daughter, to bid many beads is good for them that can do no better, but it is not perfection. Thou shalt have more merit in heaven for one year of thinking in thy mind, than for a century of praying with thy mouth." Such was her womanly tenderness for all living creatures, that "when she saw any injured, man or beast, or if she saw a man beating a child or smiting a horse with a whip, she thought she saw Our Lord Himself beaten and wounded."

After this comes a falling off, as far as can be gathered. True, we do not really know, and may never be able to know, what is passing in souls at any given period. High spirituality is apt to be secretive; it is in its very nature to be so. The mystics are the Jack Horners of religion and, in the succeeding centuries, there may have been any number of these Jack Horners. But for the purpose of history, the falling off is there. Elizabeth Barton had Fisher and More on her side, as well as her parish priest; and may God direct all parish priests, in like case, for the sake of this one. The Holy Maid of Kent had noisy and successful opponents; but some say that her retractation, as well as that of her director Dom Bocking, was engineered by Cromwell's agents. We shall know one day, but that day is not yet. There is a deep mystic strain in some of Crashaw's poems. And then there is a blank until Father Baker the Benedictine, the last of the known English mystics, who died of the plague in London in 1641. Though his style is cumbrous, his writings entitle him to a definite place in the literature of the highest spirituality. The message of his book, *Sancta Sophia*, has been summed up in a few words: "To pray is neither to talk nor to think, but rather to love."

Juliana of Norwich protested that she yielded " to our Mother Holy Church as a simple child oweth." This serves as a caution to those who picture these mystics as free-lance religionists with nothing "churchy" about them. Christian prayer, even the most sublime expressions of it, has always been conducted according to some plan; just as surely as Christian mysticism, even the most profound, operates within the framework of some definite theology. Because the spirit bloweth where it listeth, this is not to say that the said spirit pays no heed whatever to principles and order. The entire history of the phenomenon proves the very reverse. Submission to dogmas and established rules can restrict spiritual genius no more than the genius of the artist. In fact, we may apply to mysticism what Baudelaire wrote concerning the principles of poetry. " It is clear that systems are not forms of tyranny arbitrarily devised to prevent originality from manifesting itself; rather do they assist the development of originality."

A CLOUD OF WITNESSES

THE Catholic authorities have gathered together the names of over three hundred of their fellow countrymen who, between 1535 and 1681, gave their lives here in England and Wales for the old faith and the old Roman allegiance. To the majority of these, official recognition, including the highest, has already been accorded. And all of them are usually listed together under the denomination of English Martyrs. Protestants generally might be willing enough to extend their sympathy to these victims, did they not find themselves pulled up by the recollection that they have victims of their own, and victims, moreover, for whose fate a Catholic Queen was mainly responsible. Up and down the land, one comes across their monuments; and it must be conceded that the treatment meted out to them has done much to alienate the goodwill of our non-Catholic fellow countrymen. What we have on our hands, therefore, is the one big question of religious toleration involving historical issues of a very complex character. These, obviously, could not be discussed in a superficial work of this kind, so that we shall content ourselves with quoting the statement made by a modern Catholic writer of repute.

"Catholics, however much they appreciate the intimate connection of Church and State in the medieval period, cannot but grieve that zeal for objective values in religion and society should have sometimes weakened men's understanding of personal values. They cannot but grieve that pure logic restricted the power of psychological sympathy, so that men sometimes were blind to several of the most luminous teachings of the Gospel, as for instance, to the teaching that the Kingdom of God is not of this world and is not a kingdom of the sword, and that fire should not be invoked from heaven upon unbelieving cities." [1]

[1] Karl Adam in *The Spirit of Catholicism*.

And there is no call, in a work of this description, to traverse the painful story of their sufferings and death. The greater number were hanged, some of them in chains; others were beheaded, including Thomas More, John Fisher, Margaret Pole, Adrian Fortescue, and Thomas Percy; several were starved to death in gaol, and several others strangled; Margaret Clitherow was crushed under a weighted door. Nicholas Owen succumbed to torture; the Earl of Arundel died while a prisoner under sentence. John Forest was burned, and Robert Price was shot by Puritan soldiers.

Of the three hundred and more whose sacrifice has so far been officially acclaimed by the Holy See, two hundred and twenty-two were priests, the majority being secular priests. Over seventy were members of religious orders, and to these must be added a fair number of lay-brothers. The Carthusian, Blessed John Houghton, who was an Essex man, has the signal honour of being the very first, since pagan times, to suffer death in England for being a Catholic. Seventeen of his brethren shared his fate. The Benedictines include the Abbots of Colchester, Glastonbury, and Reading. Many belonged to the Society of Jesus. A round dozen were Franciscans, including John Forest, Queen Catherine's confessor. The laity, of whom four were women, make up a good part of the total. Of these laity, the first to suffer was John Felton, a citizen of London, who fastened a copy of the Pope's Bull, excommunicating Elizabeth, to the door of the Bishop of London's house; a daring, but not in itself a seditious proceeding, since the Act that made such a gesture treasonable was not passed until the following year.

The proto-martyr, that is to say the aforementioned John Houghton, was indicted for refusing to acknowledge Henry's Act of Supremacy which became law the year before; the last was William Howard, Viscount Stafford, beheaded on Tower Hill for alleged complicity in the so-called plot of the perjurer Titus Oates. Between these two dates, 1535 and 1680, is a succession of witnesses belonging to every rank and class in the community.

John Storey was a Doctor of Law, Thomas More had been Speaker of the House of Commons and Lord Chancellor, John Fisher was a bishop and a cardinal, Richard Langhorne was a barrister, Edward Coleman was secretary to the Duchess of York, Peter Wright was a military chaplain in the Civil War. The higher nobility are represented by Thomas Percy and Philip Howard, both of whom were Earls. Thomas Dingley and David Gonson were Knights of St. John, as also was Adrian Fortescue, Anne Boleyn's cousin, of whom it has been said that all the military glories of the nation were his by right of inheritance—Hastings, the Crusades and Agincourt. Margaret Pole, Countess of Salisbury, was a Plantagenet of the Royal House of England, and a near relative of Henry VIII. Between eighty and ninety belonged to the two universities, of whom most were Oxford men.

And pretty well every part of the country provided its quota. Thomas More was a Londoner bred and born, as were the priests Thomas Garnet, Edmund Campion, John Lowe, Edward Waterson, and Hugh Green. The earlier victims belonged mostly to the south and west of England, which were the first localities to feel the pressure of the new enactments ; but when the turn of the midlands and north did come, the response was a very proud one. Lancashire's record is particularly remarkable, all the more so when it is remembered that that county, now the most populous of the English shires, was in the sixteenth century among the most sparsely populated of them all.

Considering their number, detailed information regarding these men and women is very scanty indeed. St. Thomas More and St. John Fisher are notorious exceptions, and a certain number of interesting facts have been brought to light concerning the character of Blessed Edmund Campion and some others. But it would be difficult to compile anything in the nature of a full-length biography of any of the remainder. The political situation at the time, and for long after, made the preservation, and even compilation, of records an extremely hazardous business. Thus, for example, in 1643, the Archbishop of Cambrai, at the instance of the Holy See, commissioned certain English priests to act as intelligence officers. They were to tour the country and gather up all the information they could find relative to the life and sufferings of those who had been put to death. But the very documents sent into England by the archbishop fell into the hands of the civil authorities, who promptly printed and published them. On the very day of this publication, one of the priests appointed was arrested and subsequently executed at Tyburn.

Mostly, what we get is a very meagre account of the martyr's parentage, early life and education, followed by a lengthy recital of facts relating to the arrest, the trial, the condemnation and the death. In some instances even these latter are wanting. The Abbots of Colchester, Glastonbury, and Reading, along with four of their fellow monks, were executed in the reign of Henry VIII. At the time, those most concerned to know what they were charged with were not able to find out ; and little or nothing has come to light since. For some reason or other, the official records of the indictment of these seven are missing, with the result that biographers have had to rely on second-hand and hostile sources.

The legal case against the majority was clear-cut and decisive ; they were found guilty of conduct which certain Acts of Parliament adjudged to be treasonable and capital offences. Under Henry, for example, one such Act was directed against those who might deny the validity of the King's new marriage, and another against all who refused to acknowledge him as supreme head of the Church in England. About fifty martyrs suffered under these two enactments. When Elizabeth came to the throne, farther and similar Acts were passed, one of which prohibited the Mass, and another made it treason to call the Queen a heretic, or to introduce Papal Bulls, etc. The measure taken against the Mass provoked the Northern Rising, which was followed by wholesale executions. Then, in 1593, an Act went through designed for the better discovery of wicked and seditious persons calling themselves Catholics, the result being some sixty fresh victims. James I's reign was inaugurated by a law for the due execution of the statutes against Jesuits and seminary priests; while the Gunpowder Plot provided a new Oath of Allegiance impossible for Catholics. From the accession of Charles I onwards the persecution is the act of the Protestant majority forcing its will upon the sovereign. Strangely enough, under the Commonwealth there were only two executions, while of the two dozen that occurred in the reign of Charles II, more than one-half were on account of the Oates plot.

There is evidence that in some cases, particularly in the seventeenth century, the judges were personally reluctant to do what the law obliged them to do. John Southworth, whose body lies in Westminster Cathedral, was more than once arrested and set free. After his final apprehension, he was tried at the Old Bailey. He had rooms at Clerkenwell, but he frequently visited the plague-stricken dwellings of Westminster in order to attend the dying. This was well-known to everybody, including the Recorder of London, before whom he appeared. It seems likely that had he thrown upon the prosecution the onus of proving that he was a priest, he might have escaped death. However, he insisted on pleading guilty to being what he was, and was condemned. He was allowed to make a long speech at the gallows, and his remains were handed over to the Duke of Norfolk's family. The Benedictine, Father George Gervase, was another who was brought before the Recorder of London. At his trial, his attitude was very uncompromising. It was urged that the oath he was asked to take was merely an oath of loyalty which some of his own brethren, including the archpriest, had taken. His answer to that was that the said oath was more than an oath of loyalty. The Recorder next asked him did he really believe that the Pope had power to depose King James. After much urging, he replied: " Since you wish me to tell the truth, I say that the Pope can depose Kings and Emperors who deserve it." This reply caused consternation in the court.

It may be recalled that the last of the English Martyrs, Viscount Stafford, was cross-examined on this very matter, and gave a different reply. The fact is that the action of Pius V in excommunicating Elizabeth and in absolving her subjects from their allegiance, coupled with the Spanish Armada which was construed in connection with the Pope's Bull, created serious difficulties for contemporary English Catholics. At any rate, to the charge that the Church obliged him to believe that excommunicated princes might lawfully be deposed and even murdered, Stafford answered that such murdering was regarded by the Church herself as contrary to God's law, and furthermore that there were as many learned Catholic divines against the deposing power of the Papacy as for it; and that, in any case, no one had ever pretended that this latter power was a point of Catholic faith. The Viscount's acquittal was a near thing, and it is doubtful if many or any of the fifty-five peers who voted for his death really believed in his guilt. Nor, apart from the factionists, did the people at large; for when, on the scaffold, the old man protested his innocence, the crowd with one accord shouted : " We believe you, my Lord."

Another whose fate was sincerely regretted by the common people was Nicholas Postgate, executed at York the year before Stafford. He was eighty-two at the time, and for fifty years had lived in the merest hovel in the midst of the wild moor that covers the north-east corner of Yorkshire. He had made a vow of poverty; so that what he received in alms, over and above his own scanty fare, he gave to the poor. Pilgrims flocked to his cell from all quarters, and many sinners were converted by the simple sight of his voluntary privations. Thomas Ward, the controversialist, resided not far off, and paid this tribute to his friend :

> A thatched cottage was his all,
> Where this contemplative did dwell ;
> Two miles from Mulgrave Castle 't stood,
> Sheltered by snowdrifts, not by wood ;
> Tho' there he lived to that great age
> It was a dismal heritage ;
> But God placed here that saint's abode
> For Blackmoor's far greater good.

The simplicity of this priest's life, and the circumstances of his death at so advanced an age, made a deep impression on the minds of his generation, and left a memory which still endures. He loved flowers and, according to a tradition, he first brought the daffodil to that part of the country. As late as the beginning of last century, the bulbs which he planted in the garden of his hermitage were still blooming.

It was made treason to aid and abet a Catholic priest in the discharge of his ministry, and many went to the scaffold under this head. Mrs. Anne Line, for instance, allowed her house to be used for the celebration of Mass. On Candlemas Day, 1601, the priest-catchers broke into her apartments and found an altar ready prepared. She was tried at the Old Bailey three weeks later and suffered the following morning. So, too, Margaret Clitherow, the Pearl of York. Though her husband was an Anglican, she kept priests hidden through the worst of the persecution. At the assizes, she refused to plead, since the only witnesses against her would be her own little children and servants whom she refused to involve in the guilt of her fate. She walked barefooted to her death, having sent her shoes and stockings to her daughter Anne in token that she should follow in her mother's steps.

The term aiding and abetting seems, however, to have been very rigorously interpreted, for we hear tell of one Yorkshireman being executed for giving a priest a pot of ale; of another, for saving a priest's life; and of quite a number whose sole offence, apparently, was that they had given divers hungry clergymen something to eat. James Duckett and William Carter were booksellers who were hanged for printing Catholic books; Thomas Webley suffered a similar fate for distributing them.

As for the priests, some of them defied the judges to prove that they had ever exercised their ministry in England. But it made no difference. Henry Heath, the Franciscan, having been ordained abroad, made the crossing from Dunkirk to Dover and then walked to London, where he arrived late at night. Being exhausted, he lay down in the shelter of a shop-porch in Cheapside and promptly went to sleep. He was arrested where he was and went to Tyburn in due course. Thomas Sherwood was not a priest at all, but he had made up his mind to be one. He was taken on the way to Douai and condemned for his intention.

However, there was one amongst them who aided and abetted to such purpose that it is doubtful if the task of keeping alive the old faith could have been carried on without him. This was Nicholas Owen, the Jesuit lay-brother, who was mainly responsible for the manufacture of the priests' hiding holes. A builder or carpenter by trade, he devoted his craftsmanship to the service of the outlawed clergy. Up and down the country he went, with his bag of tools, spending a week in this place and a week in that, and leaving behind in each house something quite new in the shape of a secret chamber. For, of course, the very essence of the business was that there should be no repetitions and, therefore, nothing which, if discovered, might provide a clue for elsewhere. The most unlikely spots were selected. Sometimes a window-seat would conceal a trap-door leading under the floor, sometimes advantage would be taken of the chimney wall covered by the oak carving of the mantelpiece. We are told of Nicholas Owen that he never began any work of this kind without first receiving the Sacraments, and the tradition is that he it was who planned Father Gerard's amazing escape from the Tower of London. The government spies were well aware of his activities, and great was the joy when at last he was trapped and taken in one of his own hiding-holes. He paid the penalty in due course, although he had the satisfaction of knowing that his skill and energy had saved scores of lives.

In the year 1830, a servant girl mounted on a ladder to clean the upper part of the kitchen wall of an old house. The plaster gave way under her hand and she found herself looking into a little chapel. The altar was laid out for the Sacrifice, with the vestments lying upon it and the Missal, crucifix and candlesticks in their place. But the priest who was to have offered this Mass had been hanged, drawn and quartered a century and a half before. This hiding place was at Egton in Yorkshire, and may have been the handiwork of Nicholas Owen. Meanwhile, the best hiding-place at present extant is the one at Swaston, near Cambridge. The entrance is concealed in the flooring of the staircase, and its walls are of thick stone. The one at Baddesley Clinton is a converted sewage tunnel.

But as much as on hiding-holes they relied on disguises, which means that we are not to think of these priests as moving about the country attired in anything remotely resembling ecclesiastical garb. The dangers of the time made that impossible. For the most part, their apparel was so un-clerical in appearance that some of their Continental brethren, unacquainted with the conditions in England, took exception to it. We happen to know just what one of them looked like thanks to the account of an eye-witness. "The said Holforde (Venerable Thomas Holford) is a tall, blacke, fatte, stronge man; the crown of his head balde, his beard all shaven except the moustache; his apparel a blacke cloake with mulberry lace, open at the shoulders, a straw-coloured fustian doublet laide on with red lace, the buttons red, cut and laide under with red taffeta; and coloured hose laide on with lace trimmings; a little black hatte lined with velvet in the brim, a flat cambric collar and yellow knitted socks." But this turnout was almost monastic in comparison with that of others, for we hear tell of those who were so pricked out with ruffs and feathers that they passed for swash-buckling young bloods.

Unlike Master Bernardine in *Measure for Measure*, who would not get up to be hanged, these men and women displayed an extraordinary alacrity. Father Southwell wrote demanding to be either executed at once or acquitted; to which Cecil tartly replied that he would not be kept waiting long. At the last, they had very little to give away but they seldom forgot the hangman. With the noose practically round his neck, Father Everard Hanse cried out: "They should laugh that win." John Kemble was taken under guard to Hereford in order to be tried. Presently,

8

they came in sight of the city. "There," said the officer in charge, "is the place where you shall die!" "Very well," replied the martyr, "let us sit down and look at it while we smoke a pipe." In that part, for long after, the phrase *Kemble's Pipe* was a synonym for constancy. "Do your job neatly, for I've been a neat man all my life," this was Thomas Reynolds' parting word to the hangman. On being summoned to take her trial, Margaret Clitherow amused everybody in sight by making a representation of a gallows with her fingers.

And, in general, this seems to have been one notable feature of their character, a courage which had something genial and even mischievous about it. With characteristic exaggeration G. K. Chesterton maintained that his countrymen have not laughed heartily since the Middle Ages. This playfully stern indictment perhaps rather ignores the grim actualities of the medieval scene. There was certainly nothing particularly gay about the England that William Langland describes; and, indeed, the term Merrie England must be construed with due regard to the fact that, in olden times, the adjective in question did not always refer to the mood and demeanour of human beings, but rather to the physical aspect of the landscape. At all events, Chesterton's stricture would seem to ignore the English Martyrs, none of whom can fairly be called medievalists. And they were certainly a merry band, with something positively Chestertonian about them. Edmund Campion challenged Beza, Calvin's successor at Geneva, to a debate on religion, the loser to be burnt at the stake. Surely this is nothing if not in the full-blooded style of G. K.

"Take piety and learning for your meat, and play for your sauce." This was the advice Thomas More gave to the members of his large family. He certainly acted upon it himself. There was about his character a boyish spirit of fun which he carried with him to prison, and even to the scaffold. The word merry was a great favourite of his, and with him it appears to have passed out of common use. On being first warned that he might suffer death if he did not conform to the new opinion, he replied that a man might very easily lose his head and yet come to no harm. "When I complain, just turn me out of doors," was his rejoinder to the lieutenant of the Tower who apologized for the poorness of the fare. He asked to be helped up the ladder, saying that he would shift for himself at his coming down ; and he reassured the rather timid executioner : " Pluck up thy spirits, man, my neck is very short."

As Blessed David Lewis lay in prison at Monmouth, the report ran round that he had tried to poison his gaoler. The martyr himself has told the story of how this rumour originated. " He (the gaoler), coming to my chamber one night, when he was already fully drunk, insisted on drinking a pot of ale with me, whereupon I filled for him a glass of surfeit water which I had and put in a little brandy. He then went out and told his wife that I had given him such a dose that he found himself swelling to the bursting of his very buttons. She thereupon set up a loud cry that was bruited abroad. And thus did I poison my gaoler, a story which ran over four or five counties and took its flight to London itself."

We shall take leave of these martyrs by appending an anecdote which will probably appeal to everybody, whether friend or foe. Father Robert Southwell and the Earl of Arundel were in the Tower of London at the same time and, more or less, for the like offence. The latter had his dog with him, it appears, and this used to pay visits to the priest's chamber whenever it got the chance ; which occasioned the Earl to say that he loved the animal all the better for it. The lieutenant of the Tower scoffingly suggested that the dog no doubt came thither to get the priest's blessing ; to which the Earl rejoined that it was no new thing for irrational creatures to seek a blessing at the hands of saintly men.

AFTERMATH

The first comprehensive collection of English saints ever made is usually referred to as Capgrave. However, this fifteenth-century friar, who was one of the most cultivated men of his time, was only the editor of this work, its actual compiler being a Benedictine monk named John of Tynemouth, who was born many years before. The title of the book is *New Legends of England*, from which we moderns will naturally infer that it is just another sample of the medieval craze for sensationalism in the guise of the miraculous. This is not the case, however. Capgrave was a genuine scholar concerned to give us the facts as far as they could be known.

In truth, the word legend, as originally used by Christians, was quite a respectable one, and simply meant something that ought to be read, this something being the doings of sainted personages whose recital in the office of the day was a matter of obligation. The public, however, is seldom content with the truth relating to its heroes. In passing from mouth to mouth, the fact tends to be so enlarged-upon and distorted as to be quite altered out of all serious shape. It was this chronic and very natural tendency that later earned for the word legend the meaning which it conveys to our modern minds.

To Capgrave and his contemporaries, therefore, the title *Legends of the Saints* was the equivalent of the title *Lives of the Saints*. They do not, indeed, disdain the miraculous. Far from it. In that respect they were men of their age. They take the marvellous tales in their stride, just as Livy takes in his stride the marvellous tales associated with the founding of Rome, It was primarily the ethical aspect of history that appealed to Livy, and he respected the myths because he thought they possessed a symbolic truth and a moral value. Livy is, above all, a moralizing historian. But the writers of the Middle Ages were, above all, moralizing biographers ; and, to point the moral, they had recourse to the folk-lore that had grown up around the memory of their religious heroes.

The great medieval exponent or exploiter of this folk-lore was Jacopo de Voragine, whose classic work *Legenda Aurea* came to be so called because the people considered it worth its weight in gold. But this Jacopo was a most estimable person and was, in fact, beatified after his death. If we are to judge the *Golden Legend* from a strictly historical angle, we must condemn it out of hand. But the object of the man who compiled it, and of others like him, was to provide the faithful with a book not of biography but of devotion ; and he achieved his object in most triumphant fashion. He tells his tall stories solely with a view to illustration, much as the preacher of to-day might round off a point by means of this or that fable from Æsop. The *Golden Legend* is largely a work of imagination, but so, too, is the *Pilgrim's Progress* ; and if Jacopo mixes together fact and fiction, that is exactly what Dante does in his immortal poem.

It has been well said that the saints are exacting masters who never release their hold over their devotees. The tenacity of this hold is seen in the splendour of their shrines—in the gorgeousness, say, of the churches built over the remains of poor friars like St. Francis of Assisi and St. Anthony of Padua. But it is seen also in a certain headstrong eagerness to credit any popular saint with preternatural powers ; for this eagerness springs from the same restless, ardent, creative devotion. Just this is the characteristic of such devotion—a refusal to be satisfied, to tire, to believe that it has gone far enough. If legends are prone to take great liberties, this is especially true of the Middle Ages when devotion was so free and easy, when a certain amount of horse-play entered into religious behaviour.

While it must be admitted that a strong faith in Christianity does create a bias or predisposition in favour of the miraculous— as Cardinal Newman pointed out—we are not to suppose that the easy digestion of these marvellous tales on the part of our forefathers was due *entirely* to their acceptance of Catholicism. On the contrary, scholars of repute have described it as a hangover from the Hellenistic Age.

However that may be, the medievalists generally were very willing indeed to credit with extraordinary powers those whom they regarded as holy persons. These holy persons might not have done anything in that way while they were alive, but signs and wonders were to be expected of them as soon as they had passed to their reward. The merest rumour was enough to set the ball rolling. It was reported, for instance, that a curse lay upon Becket's assassins in consequence of which their descendants were born with tails. And why not? St. Patrick turned Vereticus the King of Wales into a werewolf, and St. Natalis of Kilnaile so effectively cursed an illustrious Irish family that each member of it was doomed to be a werewolf for seven years. So the old legends ran; and, consequently, for the descendants of Becket's murderers it ought to be tails at the very least. And not for them only, because a later report brought every man in the county under the malediction. Andrew Marvell, Milton's colleague, testifies that this story was current in his time.

> For Becket's sake
> Kent always shall have tails.

Addison refers to the tradition in his Essay entitled *The Grinning Match*. "A Warwickshire man," he says, "will be known by his grin, as Roman Catholics imagine a Kentish man is by his tail." A widely prevalent conviction even extended the curse to the entire nation; for, as we have already noted, among the affronts and insults bandied about by the students of Paris University was one to the effect that the English were drunkards and had tails. It was little to the purpose that nobody had actually seen the tails; those endowed with such appendages are not likely to flaunt them before the public gaze.

We shall not debate the question as to whether our credulity is less or greater than that of the ancients. Some would say that the only thing that has really changed is the direction which the credulity takes. At the worst, the medievalist seems to have regarded the person and life of the saint as fair game for the fancy ; until, at last, the historical and the mythical came to be inextricably confounded. There is nothing very vicious or harmful about this. We should be rather badly off without the myths of the ancients or the fairy-tales of later times ; and these myths and fairy-tales represent the evolution of history into poetry. St. So-and-So was credibly reported to have healed the sick and calmed the tempest, on such and such occasions. Very well ; evidently God arms His chosen servants with power over the forces of life and of nature. Starting from this premise, the legend then proceeded to represent the saint as more or less wading knee-deep in omens, portents and hair-raising experiences generally. It was imagination, but it was imagination whose working material was something authentic. And from this they derived the same satisfaction that we derive from the *Arabian Nights*, or as the Jews derive from the folk-lore of the *Talmud*.

The legends apart, many of the miracles ascribed to the intercession of our Anglo-Norman saints are no different from those ascribed to saints generally, or from those alleged to take place in modern times, say at the shrine of our Lady of Lourdes. Well enough authenticated would seem to be the report that while Becket's mangled body lay in the choir, the right hand raised itself and made the sign of the cross in benediction over the collected multitude. His eyes also, dislodged by the fury of the murderers, were believed to have been replaced by two others smaller in size and of different colours. One of the first of the prodigies wrought through the saint's intercession was in favour of a poor man, who had had his eyes put out for stealing a whetstone—a grim enough sample of the brutality of the age. For this reason or, perhaps, on account of the miracle of his own eyes, Thomas was for long regarded by the English as the special patron and protector of the blind.

Well authenticated, too, is the cure of the heir to the throne of France which took place nine years after the martyrdom. Bossuet naturally instances this miracle in his panegyric on St. Thomas. The heir in question was Philip, afterwards surnamed Augustus, the son of Louis VII. Being brought to the point of death by a mortal malady, his father was, for three nights running, advised in a dream to make a pilgrimage to Canterbury. He did so against the advice of his courtiers, and was conducted to the tomb of the martyr by Henry II himself. On his return to France, he found his son perfectly recovered; "a miraculous circumstance," says Bossuet, "to which we owe St. Louis and all those kings who are descended from this prince."

Among the numerous miracles ascribed to St. Richard Wyche is one relating to the salt wells of his native place; these dried up, but he made them flow again as profitably as ever. Another human and friendly intervention is that of St. Edmund Rich in favour of his own secretary whose raging toothache he cured at the first invocation. In the matter of raising dead people to life, St. William of York seems to have been trusted more than any other. While he was yet alive, his mere blessing had snatched a great multitude from certain death; and doubtless this was long remembered. This miracle took place when he was entering York to take possession of his cathedral. The bridge over the Ouse, in the centre of the city, collapsed under the weight of the sight-seers and the river was filled with screaming and struggling people. But the saint's benediction saved their lives.

The Thaumaturgus of the English Martyrs would seem to be Edmund Arrowsmith, who was betrayed by a member of his own faith and executed at Lancaster in 1628. One of his hands is preserved in St. Oswald's Church at Ashton-in-Makerfield in Lancashire. This relic began to be associated with miraculous cures less than a century after the priest's death. They appear to be well established and, in one instance at least, the attestation was signed by several Protestant witnesses. When the process of canonization was compiled in 1874, mention was made of twenty different miracles. And these alleged cures continue at the present day. Until quite recently, as many as twenty to sixty sick persons made their way to Ashton-in-Makerfield every week.

It goes without saying that each of these saints had his or her shrine ; the popular veneration and the artistic bent of the Middle Ages saw to that. The most famous of all was that of St. Thomas Becket, which boasted a magnificent *ex voto* in the shape of the royal diamond given by King Louis of France. For more than three centuries, all English roads led to Canterbury. When old London Bridge was removed, the dredgers brought to light quite a number of the tokens coveted by the pilgrims, brooches for fitting to the cap and showing an effigy of the archbishop with mitre and crozier, and medallions exhibiting the head only and inscribed *Caput Thomae*. The very horses used on the journey had special bells engraven with the words *Campana Thomae*.

It was Cranmer who allowed the shrine to be desecrated and plundered ; and it was he who ordered the tombs of all the canonized archbishops to be destroyed. Under him, the two great monasteries of Christ Church and St. Augustine were suppressed and confiscated. Thus did Henry VIII take it out of " that traitor Becket " as he used to call the martyr. The city never recovered from these spoliations, but the cathedral still stands as a witness to its former glory. The fate of the saint's remains is somewhat uncertain, but there are those who believe that a skeleton found in the crypt in 1888 is his skeleton.

Becket's tomb was the work of Walter of Colchester, and its jewelled fragments, when broken up by royal command, filled twenty-six carts. This and similar depredations have been excused ; but they were the acts of a man who, as Professor Chambers points out, " destroyed more things of beauty than any other man in European history." There seems to be no real evidence that this crowned philistine was ever a patron of the arts. On his accession, he inherited both funds and plans for completing his predecessor's tomb and chapel in Westminster Abbey. He embezzled the funds and mutilated the plans. Had he been honest, that chapel would now be almost without a rival. What quarrel he could have had with Edward the Confessor does not appear, but he pillaged his shrine. And the worst of it was, he set a sort of fashion in sheer destructiveness. What he left undone, the Roundheads methodically completed. And so a writer of our day affirms that this barbarian it was who knocked the heart out of the English artist.

Some five hundred miles to the north there was another monument of Becket which fared even worse than Canterbury. This is Arbroath Abbey, begun to be built eight years after the murder, and founded by William the Lion in honour of the martyr with whom the Scottish King had been on terms of personal friendship. The monarch himself was buried in the eastern portion of the noble church. This had a choir of three bays and a nave of nine, with side aisles, two transepts, a central and two western towers. It was colonized from Kelso by those Benedictine monks whose habit Becket was wearing when he met his death. Later, these constructed a fine harbour and fixed a bell on the Inchcape Rock. Of the monastery, once one of the most opulent in all Scotland, hardly a stone remains upon a stone. The ruins of the church stand up gaunt and almost terrifying. As for the sleepy little seaport itself, nowadays its sole title to fame is derived from its most excellent smoked haddocks.

St. Margaret was buried beside her husband in Dunfermline Abbey. Their tombs can still be seen in the ruined Lady Chapel of the Church. Even these might have gone to wrack and ruin had it not been for Queen Victoria, who caused them to be repaired and enclosed. According to one account, Margaret's attachment to her husband persisted even in the grave ; for when, in Catholic days, they tried to move her coffin to the new shrine, it turned into a dead weight against which neither muscles nor pulleys could avail. The monks were nonplussed, but at length it was suggested that the Queen was refusing to be parted from the King. And so it proved for, as soon as his coffin had been got out, hers resumed its normal weight and the transfer was effected. To-day, both sepulchres are empty. The bodies were salvaged, just in the nick of time, when John Knox's liege-men destroyed the splendid church, all but the nave, which is now used as a Presbyterian place of worship. By some means or other, the remains of the royal pair were transported to Spain and reinterred in the Escorial. Last century, application was made by the Catholic bishops for their restoration, but by that time, it seems, all trace of them had disappeared. It is not too much to hope that, one day, Margaret will once again, and for the last time, land upon the shores of the country which gave her hospitality some eight hundred and eighty years ago.

The humble stone coffin in which St. Wulstan was laid to rest is still shown in the presbytery or chancel of his cathedral at Worcester, the crypt and early Norman portions of which are his work.

Seven years after his death, in the presence of Queen Blanche and St. Louis, the body of St. Edmund Rich was disinterred and found to be entire and with the joints still flexible. The tomb was opened again in the seventeenth century, and the remains examined by Edmond Marténe, the Benedictine scholar. He deposes that they showed no signs of corruption. This sort of miraculous phenomenon is familiar enough in saints' lives. Some reject the miracle, and will not accept even the phenomenon. And yet, doubtless they would accept the phenomenon of Shelley's corpse which was cremated on the sea-shore after being drenched with oil and wine. "What surprised us all," Trelawny writes, "was that the heart remained entire. In snatching this relic from the fiery furnace, my hand was severely burned."

Edmund's body still reposes behind the high altar at Pontigny Abbey which came to be known, and deservedly, as the cradle of bishops and the asylum of great men. Although women were not allowed to enter Cistercian churches, an exception was made in favour of the English in the case of this sanctuary. At Pontigny, too, were preserved his episcopal ring, chalice, paten and chasuble. Pity it is that his relics lie so far away in exile, a permanent re-minder to us that he was one of whom his country was not worthy.

Pity, and yet, no pity; for Pontigny has preserved what Canterbury would most certainly have destroyed. Notable relics of the saint are treasured at Westminster Cathedral and at the great seminary of the archdiocese near Ware. His ancient Mass, taken from the Sarum Missal, is still used in the Catholic diocese of Portsmouth.

As pilgrims to Lourdes may remember, the tomb of Simon Stock rests in the cathedral of Bordeaux, in which city he died at the age of one hundred. Bordeaux was for long the capital of our English possessions in France, and many of its archbishops were conspicuous as agents of English policy. What efforts, if any, have been made for the return of the remains of this saint to his native Kent, we do not know.

Thomas of Hereford died in Italy, but his relics were brought back to his cathedral and, almost at once, the shrine became second in popularity to that of Thomas of Canterbury. Some of them were saved at the Reformation, and are now at the great Jesuit college of Stonyhurst, near Blackburn. Some others seem to have remained behind at Hereford; for, as late as 1610, we hear tell of them being carried in procession by the people during the plague—which shows that what has been bred in the bone will insist on coming out in the flesh.

In 1284 the relics of St. William of York were solemnly enshrined in the minster in presence of Edward I and his whole court. Butler says that a table, showing a copy of an indulgence of one hundred and fifty days granted to all who devoutly visit the tomb, is still to be seen in the vestry. In the sixteenth century, of course, everything of value was carried off by the looters and the saint's bones deposited in the nave under a marble stone. They were seen in 1732 when the ground was opened and, presumably, are still there.

St. Godric died at Finchale or Finkley, three miles from Durham, one of whose bishops built a chapel to his memory. Where the bones of this patron of all hawkers and peddlers now actually repose has, however, quite escaped our investigation.

Chichester, for long, gloried in the splendid tomb of St. Richard Wyche, but its liquidation and that of its contents appear to have been complete. Gilbert was, of course, buried in the church of Sempringham, and may be still there. John of Bridlington continued to be so popular in the North that, when Henry VIII cast covetous eyes upon his magnificent shrine, the inhabitants petitioned him to stay his hand. But the King was not the sort of man to pay attention to such petitions, even had they been signed by the three Persons of the Blessed Trinity. The said shrine was picked clean on pretence that it was inviting offerings which the people could ill afford to make. " Now Judas said this, not because he cared for the poor but because he was a thief."

Of the English Martyrs comparatively few relics remain, and these are mostly minor ones. In general, it was part of the policy of those who condemned them, to see that their bodies did not fall into the hands of their followers. The preservation of the head of St. Thomas More was due to the courage and devotion of his daughter, and this sort of thing was a rare occurrence, particularly in the beginning. It was only towards the end of the persecution that the vigilance was relaxed. Thus, the authorities allowed the remains of Blessed Oliver Plunket to be gathered up by his Catholic brethren and interred in the churchyard of St. Giles. This Irishman was Archbishop of Armagh, and his martyrdom in 1681 closed the long series of executions for the Faith.

The wasted body of St. John Fisher was shamefully ill-treated even in death. For a whole day, it lay where it had fallen " as a spectacle to the people." Towards evening it was tumbled into a shallow hole in All Hallows' Churchyard, Barking, without rites or shroud. For two weeks his head remained upon London Bridge, after which it was thrown into the river to make room for that of St. Thomas More. This latter passed into the keeping of the martyr's favourite daughter Meg, and is thought to lie in the Roper vault at St. Dunstan's, Canterbury ; but where the body is it is impossible to say for certain, although some think that it lies under the pavement of Chelsea Old Church, which was destroyed in the air raids on London. The Jesuit Fathers of Stonyhurst College possess his hat, cap, gold crucifix, silver seal, and other articles. His hair shirt is preserved in the convent of the Augustinian Canonesses at Abbots Leigh, Devonshire.

Blessed Margaret Clitherow was buried in a foul dunghill near the city walls; but, soon after, the remains were recovered by the Catholics of York and reinterred in a safe place a long way off. The secret of the new grave was so well kept that, to this day, its whereabouts are unknown. One of the martyr's hands, however, was removed and, according to a tradition two centuries old, is preserved in a splendid reliquary at the Convent of St. Mary's just outside the Micklegate Bar in York.

The priest John Southworth was executed in 1654. The wonderful recovery, two years later, of Francis Howard, seventh son of the Earl of Arundel, was attributed to the intercession of the martyr whose remains, as we have noted elsewhere, passed into the keeping of the Duke of Norfolk. In due course, he sent them for safety across the sea to the English College at Douai. They were secreted during the French Revolution, and, for over a century, all trace of them was lost. Some years ago they were recovered, and now repose in one of the side chapels of Westminster Cathedral. This would seem to be the one and only complete relic of an English martyr whose whereabouts are known.

Considering the thoroughness with which the shrines of the English saints were destroyed during the religious change-over, it is not easy to understand why the places of worship were allowed to retain their titular names. From an exhaustive compilation published in 1899 it appears that, at that time, no fewer than two thousand one hundred and sixty-two Anglican churches were still dedicated to the Blessed Virgin. From the same we gather that the native saint most favoured as a church-dedication is St. Thomas of Canterbury and, after him, St. Cuthbert. But, in this matter, the English have never been in the least insular or exclusively national. The greater number of the Anglo-Saxon churches were dedicated to St. Peter, the Prince of the Apostles. Until the twelfth century, the Irish admitted very few foreign saints into their martyrology; but it was otherwise on this side of the Channel. In pre-Reformation days, the City of London contained over one hundred churches, but of these comparatively few were dedicated to nationals.